Oracle Database Performance Tuning Interview Questions, Answers, and Explanations: Oracle Performance Tuning FAQ

ORACOOKBOOK.COM

Please visit our website at www.oracookbook.com
© 2006 Equity Press all rights reserved.

ISBN 1-933804-64-5

TABLE OF CONTENTS

Oracle Database Performance Tuning Interview
Questions, Answers, and Explanations: Oracle
Performance Tuning FAQ.. **vii**

Question 1:   Table scan in one of many partitions............ 1
Question 2:   Numeric or Alphanumeric data type 3
Question 3:   The best way to create an index 4
Question 4:   Tuning buffer hit ratio on Oracle 8i 6
Question 5:   ORA-024012: PLAN_TABLE not found......... 7
Question 6:   Library cache latch 8
Question 7:   Select doubt 12
Question 8:   db block gets and consistent gets 13
Question 9:   Visual Explain... 16
Question 10: Attempt to de-mystify DBMS_STATS 17
Question 11: Unique constraint versus unique index...... 19
Question 12: Help with outer join..................................... 20
Question 13: Commit time format in retention table 22
Question 14: Functional index and bind
              variable problem 23
Question 15: SQL Query not using Composite Index...... 25
Question 16: Query takes a lot of time to execute........... 27
Question 17: Bad view and slow reports 33
Question 18: Statistics, to update or not.......................... 37
Question 19: Tuning: Multiple table inner join query
              with partitioning... 39
Question 20: Shrinking index table space........................ 42
Question 21: Turn logging on, on Index 43
Question 22: change snapshot timing................................ 44
Question 23: Query, using bind variable is slower........... 45
Question 24: SQL with a very slow response 47
Question 25: Tablespace increase...................................... 49

Question 26:   Explain Plan..51
Question 27:   Tuning this query...54
Question 28:   The difference between 2 execution
               method..58
Question 29:   Why AWR doesn't collect statistics
               information 62
Question 30:   Issue in temporary tablespace....................63
Question 31:   force a hash join..64
Question 32:   Indexes Difference.......................................67
Question 33:   Prove plan invalidations...............................71
Question 34:   To see the optimized SQL by CBO 75
Question 35:   AUM in Oracle 76
Question 36:   Use of PCTfree, Initran, and Maxtran to
               prevent contention.......................................77
Question 37:   Procedure tuning...80
Question 38:   bigger block size for indexes help
               increase performance and lower I/O 81
Question 39:   Tuning SQL by using explain plan...............83
Question 40:   "slave shutdown wait" – event 90
Question 41:   Oracle 9i function base index......................91
Question 42:   Query tuning with NVL.................................96
Question 43:   Checkpoint is running slow 99
Question 44:   Users and default optimizer_mode...........100
Question 45:   Rewrite a query 101
Question 46:   Production database to test
               environment for load tests.........................105
Question 47:   Foreign key vs. Custom Scripts.................106
Question 48:   Full table scan 107
Question 49:   The best strategy to gather statistics
               in a dynamic way...110
Question 50:   Use of more disk space in
               executing query...111
Question 51:   Document security model..........................112

Question 52:   Forced view 115
Question 53:   Composite bitmap indexes 117
Question 54:   Select on some table which gives poor
               performance 120
Question 55:   Index partition rebuilds query...................124
Question 56:   Oracle server information...........................125
Question 57:   Batch tuning...126
Question 58:   Oracle problem connect by
               VB application 127
Question 59:   Archive log getting filled 128
Question 60:   Cursor performance issue...........................129
Question 61:   Max size of SGA in Oracle 8i 131
Question 62:   dbms_stats 132
Question 63:   Rollback segment error in production 135
Question 64:   Tuning question 136
Question 65:   Analyze table and index 137
Question 66:   lock_sga parameter......................................138
Question 67:   Check if index is rebuilt or not..................139
Question 68:   Disk partition strategy.................................141
Question 69:   the analyze table...142
Question 70:   no_index optimizer hint 143
Question 71:   Selecting data out of partition...................145
Question 72:   Server response degrades...........................147
Question 73:   SQL executed session wise.........................148
Question 74:   ora-02287 sequence not allowed 149
Question 75:   Performance tuning a query 151
Question 76:   Index and changing selected columns 170
Question 77:   Full table scan with varying
               consistence 173
Question 78:   Parallel hint question...................................176
Question 79:   Invalid object in sys schema......................178
Question 80:   Getting data in one pass..............................179
Question 81:   Replace outer join with union 184

Question 82:   DML on Global temp table 185
Question 83:   Getting procedure and package names 186
Question 84:   A long running query in Oracle 186
Question 85:   Execution stats shown on TOAD 187
Question 86:   Tuning SGA 188
Question 87:   Checking fragmentation 189
Question 88:   Views or tables 190
Question 89:   Connecting with oracle database 191
Question 90:   Sorting results 192
Question 91:   database is full 193
Question 92:   Explaining the explain plan 194
Question 93:   Session related queries 198
Question 94:   Oracle 8/9/10 performance problem 200
Question 95:   10g Advisor 202
Question 96:   Main use of Pmon 204
Question 97:   Analyzing SQL query 205
Question 98:   Recovery in occurrence of
               crash instance 206
Question 99:   Does remote table use remote
               indexes? 207
Question 100: Analyze table frequently 208
Index 209

Oracle Database Performance Tuning Interview Questions, Answers, and Explanations: Oracle Performance Tuning FAQ

ORACOOKBOOK
Equity Press

☞ QUESTION 1

Table scan in one of many partitions

My application uses several tables partitioned in one field from their multi-part keys. In certain partitions, full table scans are performed during operations which results in severely degrading the performance. It usually takes only 4 minutes to do the job, but now it takes 5 hours.

The statistics for this partition are updated and recomputed. However, this didn't solve the problem. Other partitions running the same jobs run quickly with no table scans. If I copy the data in the problem partition into a new partition, it doesn't exhibit the same behavior.

We recently upgraded from 10.1.0.4 to 10.2.0.1. After that, we experienced these problems in specific partitions.

Any ideas on what is wrong?

✍ ANSWER

It could be a HWM problem. If the partition was once bigger, most of its rows are deleted and you need to rebuild it. If you are on 10g, you can use the "SHRINK" clause in the "ALTER TABLE" command. Otherwise, you need to rebuild the partition as a separate table, and then use the "EXCHANGE PARTITION" clause to swap the inefficient partition out.

The best way to find out is to use "SQL*Trace" and "TK*Prof".

ALTER SESSION SET SQL_TRACE = true;
-- run slow SQL
-- run fast sql
ALTER SESSION SET SQL_TRACE = false;

Find the trace file and run "TK*Prof". Details are in the Oracle Performance Tuning manual. If the slow SQL has the same plan as the fast one, and read the same number of rows with much higher disk reads, then you almost certainly have the HWM problem.

☞ QUESTION 2

Numeric or Alphanumeric data type

In a table, I have a column named EMPID. Now I want to make EMPID as a numeric data type which has more advantage a alphanumeric data type. I received information that there will be a improvement in performance by using numeric type than alphanumeric type. Is this true?

✍ ANSWER

A numeric data type will generally take a little less space than the text equivalent in a VACHAR2 data type.

Otherwise, the advantages are you can disallow non-numeric values, and you can perform arithmetic or "SUM()/AVG()" functions without casting to a number.

The disadvantage is that you can only store integers up to about 38 significant digits. Varchar2 can store several thousand digits.

It's not a big performance consideration. Index scans and comparison operation are not noticeably faster. Unless you were scanning several million rows, the space saving of "NUMBER" over "VARCHAR2" would not translate into a considerable I/O saving.

☞ **QUESTION 3**

The best way to create an index

If I have an SQL query like:

> select a.*
> from tabA a,
> tabB b
> where a.in_dt = b.in_dt
> and a.out_dt = b.out_dt
> and a.he_dept = b.dept

Will it be better to use a composite index on tabA with the 3 attributes: "in_dt", "out_dt", and "he_dept", or 3 individual indexes?

Can you refer a useful link on this topic?

✎ **ANSWER**

For that particular query, indexes on tabA won't help unless tabA contains thousands of rows that have no match in tabB.

Assuming that matches exist for most rows, your SQL will return almost every row in tabA. An index is most useful when it is used to scan very small proportions of a table (say, <10%).

If you were to further constrain the query with something like: "AND b.colx = 'VAL'", then a composite index on the join columns of tabA will help.

Single column indexes don't help because Oracle generally cannot use a two index scan to resolve a join. There are rare exceptions but it doesn't apply to this case which is slower than a composite index.

You can also read the Oracle Performance Tuning manual for more information.

☞ **QUESTION 4**

Tuning buffer hit ratio on Oracle 8i

We have Oracle 8i on NT server.

On checking the buffer Hit ratio on our current environment, it's giving a value of 56%. I heard that this value should be around 90%.

Here is the query that I'm using:

SELECT ROUND((1-(phy.value / (cur.value +
2 con.value)))*100,2) "Cache Hit Ratio"
3 FROM v$sysstat cur, v$sysstat con, v$sysstat phy
4 WHERE cur.name = 'db block gets'
5 AND con.name = 'consistent gets'
6 AND phy.name = 'physical reads';

Is there any way of Performance Tuning to enhance this value?

For instance, if a table has a set of indexes, how can I know which particular columns of the table have the index and which ones do not?

✍ **ANSWER**

You can use the following:

INDEX_NAME	COLUMN_NAME
SYS_C001891	DEPTNO

SYS_C001892	EMPNO
MYINDEX	ENAME
MYINDEX	SAL
SYS_C001887	PK

You can look into "user_ind_columns scott@9i > select index_name,column_name from user_ind_columns;" to check for indexes.

☞ **QUESTION 5**

ORA-024012: PLAN_TABLE not found

When I try to explain the plan, it gives me the error: "ORA-024012: PLAN_TABLE not found".

Is there a way to resolve this?

✍ **ANSWER**

The table and information available changes from version to version. The performance tuning, guides you through how to configure the "plan_table". Basically, there is a script that each version of oracle provides that you can run. "utlxplan.sql", I believe is in the "rdbms/admin" folder.

Also, there is a "utlxplan.sql" file either in oracle directory or you can download from google. Just run that file and it will solve your problem.

☞ QUESTION 6

Library cache latch

During peaks of activity on a production database, all my application ceased.

Statspack reports showed me latch free problems, and particularly library cache.

library cache	kglpndl: child: before pro	0	2,646	3,298
library cache	kglpndl: child: after proc	0	2,053	42
library cache	kglhdgn: child:	0	1,473	2,568
library cache	kglpnp: child	0	1,231	2,094

I don't know if it's an application problem or a bad parameter.

I traced a specific application to understand what happen in the session level:

INSERT INTO PRIX_PRODUIT (PRODUIT, DATE, PRIX, NOMBRE)
VALUES
(:B6 , :B5 , :B4 , :B3 , :B2 , :B1)

call	count	cpu	elapsed	disk	query	current	rows
Parse	0	0.00	0.00	0	0	0	0
Execute	48372	15.47	245.57	875	3383	750261	48372
Fetch	0	0.00	0.00	0	0	0	0
total	48372	15.47	245.57	875	3383	750261	48372

Misses in library cache during parse: 0
Misses in library cache during execute: 1
Optimizer goal: CHOOSE
Parsing user id: 45   (recursive depth: 1)

Elapsed times include waiting on following events:

Event waited on	Times Waited	Max. Wait	Total Waited
db file sequential read	875	0.82	22.85
latch free	377	2.90	17.20
log file switch completion	26	0.97	11.38
log file sync	925	1.27	61.87
log buffer space	36	0.97	10.17
buffer busy waits	2	0.35	0.35

****

call LOAD.SET_PRIX_PRODUIT (:1, :2, :3, :4)

call	count	cpu	elapsed	disk	query	current	rows
Parse	0	0.00	0.00	0	0	0	0
Execute	48372	9.63	77.70	4	77	149	0
Fetch	0	0.00	0.00	0	0	0	0
total	48372	9.63	77.70	4	77	149	0

Misses in library cache during parse: 0
Misses in library cache during execute: 1
Optimizer goal: CHOOSE
Parsing user id: 45

Elapsed time includes waiting on following events:

Event waited on	Times Waited	Max. Wait	Total Waited

latch free	2343	6.18	184.44
SQL*Net message to client	48372	0.00	0.07
SQL*Net message from client	48372	0.68	41.77

****

=====================
PARSING IN CURSOR #5 len=53 dep=0 uid=45 oct=170 lid=45
tim=1114550297451030 hv=1663224314 ad='b5b6a250'
call LOAD.SET_PRIX_PRODUIT (:1, :2, :3, :4, :5, :6)
END OF STMT
EXEC #5:c=0,e=99727,p=0,cr=7,cu=17,mis=1,r=0,dep=0,og=
4,tim=1114550297451025
WAIT #5: nam='latch free' ela= 981 p1=-1418751532 p2=157
p3=0
WAIT #5: nam='SQL*Net message to client' ela= 2
p1=1413697536 p2=1 p3=0
WAIT #5: nam='SQL*Net message from client' ela= 369
p1=1413697536 p2=1 p3=0
WAIT #6: nam='latch free' ela= 3511 p1=-1418751732 p2=157
p3=0

=====================

EXEC #5:c=0,e=3779739,p=2,cr=7,cu=15,mis=0,r=0,dep=0,o
g=4,tim=1114550341383273
WAIT #5: nam='latch free' ela= 14577 p1=-1418751332 p2=157
p3=0
WAIT #5: nam='latch free' ela= 157552 p1=-1418751532
p2=157 p3=0
WAIT #5: nam='SQL*Net message to client' ela= 2
p1=1413697536 p2=1 p3=0
WAIT #5: nam='SQL*Net message from client' ela= 1466
p1=1413697536 p2=1 p3=0

EXEC #5:c=0,e=79520,p=1,cr=7,cu=15,mis=0,r=0,dep=0,og=
4,tim=1114550341878306
WAIT #5: nam='latch free' ela= 7322 p1=-1418751332 p2=157
p3=0

WAIT #5: nam='SQL*Net message to client' ela= 2
p1=1413697536 p2=1 p3=0
WAIT #5: nam='SQL*Net message from client' ela= 4726
p1=1413697536 p2=1 p3=0

Why did the call of the package take a long time?

✍ ANSWER

The things that stand out are:

INSERT INTO PRIX_PRODUIT (PRODUIT, DATE, PRIX,
NOMBRE)
VALUES
 (:B6 , :B5 , :B4 , :B3 , :B2 , :B1)

call	count	cpu	elapsed	disk	query	current	rows
Parse	0	0.00	0.00	0	0	0	0
Execute	48372	15.47	245.57	875	3383	750261	48372

It's incorrect syntax on the insert. This insert was executed
48,372 times, which is identical to the calls to the package.
This may imply that the client is executing the insert one at
a time, or the insert called as a consequence of the package
call. If this is the case, there may be mileage in "bulk"-ing up
this statement.

☞ QUESTION 7

Select doubt

People choose the table with less number of rows as the driving table.

What is the reason behind this?

✍ ANSWER

Actually, it is the table with fewer rows after the filter conditions has been applied, that should be used as the driving table. The reason is that the smaller the number of rows that you are working with, the faster it can process them. The earlier the point at which you narrow down that number of rows, the quicker it will process.

If table1 has 1,000 rows and table2 has 100,000 rows, but only 10 of the rows in table2 satisfy the condition "where filter_column = some_value" and you are running the following query with appropriate indexes on the id column:

```
select table1.some_column, table2.another_column
from table1, table2
where table1.id = table2.id
and table2.filter_column = some_value;
```

Then, table2 will be your driving table, because the filter condition can limit it to 10 rows before joining to table1.

However, this is a moot issue when using the cost-based optimizer (CBO), since it will select the driving table for you.

☞ QUESTION 8

db block gets and consistent gets

When we run set auto trace on similar execution statistics, what does it mean by "db block gets" and "consistent gets"? Are they CPU bound? What do we need to do to see lower numbers?

✍ ANSWER

"Consistent gets", is the blocks in consistent mode (sometimes reconstructed using information from RBS). This reconstruction from RBS takes more resources, (reads actually) which will end up as high consistent gets.

"db block gets" is the blocks in current mode.

Your goal should be to reduce the logical i/o's (which is db block gets + consistent gets).
When you reduce LIO, your Physical I/O is reduced.

scott@9i > set autotrace traceonly statistics
scott@9i > select * from emp;
14 rows selected.

Statistics
----
      0 recursive calls
      0 db block gets
     19 consistent gets
      0 physical reads

0 redo size
1495 bytes sent via SQL*Net to client
655 bytes received via SQL*Net from client
2 SQL*Net roundtrips to/from client
0 sorts (memory)
0 sorts (disk)
14 rows processed

Open another session. Do some DML on the table. Leave the other session as is, and come back to original session. Execute again. You can see "consistent gets" is high because, it is derived using the undo information. The changes done in the other session will not be reflected in this session. To maintain this consistency, if needed, oracle will use undo information to consider only the before image (that was before the update in another session and not yet been committed).

scott@9i > /

14 rows selected.

Statistics
----
0 recursive calls
0 db block gets
34 consistent gets
0 physical reads
52 redo size
1495 bytes sent via SQL*Net to client
655 bytes received via SQL*Net from client
2 SQL*Net roundtrips to/from client
0 sorts (memory)
0 sorts (disk)
14 rows processed

Now issued a commit in other session, and then execute the SQL here. You will see "consistent gets" are back to normal.
scott@9i > /

14 rows selected.

Statistics
```
-------------------------------------------------
```
    0 recursive calls
    0 db block gets
   19 consistent gets
    0 physical reads
    0 redo size
 1462 bytes sent via SQL*Net to client
  655 bytes received via SQL*Net from client
    2 SQL*Net roundtrips to/from client
    0 sorts (memory)
    0 sorts (disk)
   14 rows processed

☞ QUESTION **9**

Visual Explain

I have an issue with optimizing/tuning RDBMS. There are a lot of options to do it. My main interest is optimizing Oracle as well as DB2. I found a tool named Visual Explain for DB2 Databases. This tool can analyze your SQL and draw you a query plan. That's a nice way for finding failures in SQL and indexes and so on.

My question now is, is there a similar tool for Oracle RDBMS too?

✍ ANSWER

If you have Oracle Enterprise Manager (OEM), there is a nice Explain Plan in the "SQL*Scratchpad" tool. You can also view the plan for currently running SQL's in the 'SESSION window'.

TOAD (downloadable off the Web) is also okay for explain plan.

Apart from TOAD, there are more tools available. Some of the excellent tools are SQL Navigator and Spot Light on Oracle. The Spot Light gives out an entire picture DB, in a graphical format which considers every corner of DB. It's more expensive though.

☞ QUESTION 10

Attempt to de-mystify DBMS_STATS

One large table is estimated to have 400 million rows (of course it's partitioned). Gather Stats on this table takes about 3 - 3.5 hrs. The table grows every 3 weeks at about 10%. The table is cleaned out and reloaded completely every three weeks.

My question is, once I gather stats on the table do I need to gather stats right from the beginning, every time I reload it?

The existing rows in the table never change, only that there will be the 10% additional rows.

So with this information, is it safe to assume that if I keep the statistics from the load three weeks before, will the queries on the new table (New size :Original Rows + 10% of original) have noticeable degradation in performance? I am trying to save the gather stats time. One more thing to note is that this table is not in an OLTP environment. It is in a Data warehouse type environment. Hence, it is not consistently hit upon for small chunks of data.

✍ ANSWER

It all depends. Unless you expect that the new records are going to change your plan drastically, you don't need to gather stats. For certain queries, partition level statistics may be useful.

If the execution plans of all your queries are stable, then

there is no need to gather stats again.

Two warnings though:

1. If you submit a query like "...AND txn_dt > 'const val'", then the column histograms from your old stats might tell you that there are no rows for this range. CBO can choose an index access in this case. If there are 10M rows in reality, an index-scan would be a bad idea. If this is a concern, gather stats at every load or do not analyze columns.

2. Oracle 10g is a clever thing. It is configured by default to capture a summary of changes to a table since the last analysis. If it sees that the table was truncated since the analysis, then I can't guarantee the CBO will not take appropriate action (which may include dynamically sampling the table during the parse).

DBA's can't control the data or the queries, so the only safe advice is to always analyze.

Another suggestion is to try tests with various percentages to see if there are any appreciable difference in either the actual statistics, hoists gathered, or plans of your most important/expensive queries.

Suggested estimate percentages would be 2, 5, 10, 15, 20, 30, and 100. Start with two tests, at 2 percent and 100 percent. If there's no difference, then stop. Otherwise, increase your percentage slowly and try again. With 400 million, you could probably get away with 1%.

If you data change is predictable, you can potentially calculate the statistic changes yourself, and manually modify the dictionary via calls to "dbms_stats.set_stats". There's no need to bother if the above approaches knock your estimate time down to a negligible amount.

☞ QUESTION 11

Unique constraint versus unique index

My application is insert intensive, and I have multiple indexes defined as unique, to ensure the there will be no duplicate values. Which case will be less for the overhead, when defining unique constraint or unique index? The indexes are not used in the select/update statements.

✎ ANSWER

The presence of index is good for select statements, and bad for inserts. If you are not using indexes in select statements, there's no need for them. An enabled unique or PK constraint, creates a unique index if it's not in existence yet. A disabled constraint requires no index, but neither is it validated. It is for documentation only.

The only differences that I know of, are a function-based index can't be a unique key, and a foreign key must refer to a unique or primary key, but a unique index is insufficient.

If you load data in bulk, you can drop your index, load, and recreate it. Depending on the data volumes, this might be beneficial. If you bulk load with 'SQL*Loader', direct path load will defer the maintenance of indexes, making it redundant (and slower) to drop and recreate them. Even better, you can pre-sort the data file in index order for a faster load.

☞ QUESTION 12

Help with outer join

I have an old view which used MAX(ID) to determine the
most recent record. The app stopped using sequences, and
replaced them with custom solution. To determine the most
recent value, I need to use the create date. I have multiple
records with the same time stamp, so I still need to go to the
MAX(ID) for the date stamp.

I have something like the query, but it doesn't bring me back
the records from the 2 tables. if there's a no match in the
third. When I put the pluses as shown bellow, then I get
Oracle error for outer join in subquery. I tried a sample like:

select a as name, (select addr1 from address where...) as
addr1, (select addr2 from addr where) addr2, etc. Is this the
best way?

    SELECT e.ent_id,n.first_name,n.last_name,
    a.addr1,a.addr2, a.addr3, a.city, a.state as state_code,
    a.postal_code, a.country as country_code
    from ent e, name n, address a
    where e.ent_id (+)= n.ent_id
    --and e.ent_id = 3
    and e.ent_id (+)= a.ent_id
    and a.addr_id =
    (select max(addr_id) from address a2
    where a2.ent_id = e.ent_id AND a2.sys_create_dt = (select
    max(a3.sys_create_dt) from address a3
    where a3.ent_id = e.ent_id))
    and n.name_id = (select max(name_id) from name n2
    where n2.ent_id = e.ent_id AND n2.sys_create_dt = (select

max(n3.sys_create_dt) from name n3
where n3.ent_id = e.ent_id))

✍ ANSWER

You need an analytic query where you can do a rank() over, (order by create date desc, sequence desc) and do it all in an inline view, with the outer condition requesting for a rank of 1. Relatively straightforward use of rank(). Check the advanced sql forum for some examples if needed.

You can also do something like:

"SELECT MAX(id) KEEP (DENSE_RANK FIRST ORDER BY txn_dt DESC)"

Note that this is an Aggregate function, not an Analytic function (as it has no OVER clause). It does an aggregate max using a restricted set of rows that have the highest "txn_dt".

☞ QUESTION **13**

Commit time format in retention table

I made a dump of an undo segment header block, to read the extent commit time in the Retention Table.

I saw this:

Retention Table

Extent Number:0 Commit Time: 1133357275
Extent Number:1 Commit Time: 1133357278
Extent Number:2 Commit Time: 1133357288
Extent Number:3 Commit Time: 1133357296
Extent Number:4 Commit Time: 1133357299
Extent Number:5 Commit Time: 1133357306
Extent Number:6 Commit Time: 1133357319
Extent Number:7 Commit Time: 1133357324
Extent Number:8 Commit Time: 1133357333
Extent Number:9 Commit Time: 1133357338

Which is the date format of Commit Time?

I was informed that the format is Julian time, but when I try to convert the "Julian string 1133357333" in the format "YYYY-MON-DD HH24:MI:SS", using select "TO_CHAR(to_date('11333573334','J'), 'YYYY-MON-DD HH24:MI:SS')" from dual, I obtained an "ora-01830 error".

✍ ANSWER

It might be "#secs since 1/1/1970 GMT". This places your data around 30/11/2005.

☞ QUESTION 14

Functional index and bind variable problem

I'm using the oracle version 8i. There is a function based index "FT_TEXT_FN_IDX on FILE_TEXT" table, which was created to improve the performance. The query below is not using this index.

Parameters
===========

query_rewrite_enabled boolean TRUE
query_rewrite_integrity string TRUSTED

SELECT TEXT FROM FI_TEXT WHERE FILE_NAME = :b1
AND TEXT LIKE :b2 AND SUBSTR(TEXT,:b3,12) = :b4

FBI script:

```
CREATE INDEX FT_TEXT_FN_IDX ON FI_TEXT
(SUBSTR("TEXT",12,12))
LOGGING
TABLESPACE CON_IDX
PARALLEL ( DEGREE 2 INSTANCES 1 );
```

In select query, I replaced bind variable ":b3" with value 12, which is exactly like, create functional index. Is there a solution to this problem?

✍ ANSWER

The query must contain a literal value. Since the CBO comes up with an execution plan at 'PARSE', which occurs before the bind, oracle does not know that you will use 12.

Oracle allows cursor sharing if everything is the same, but the bind values. This means that every execution has the same execution plan, regardless of the bind values. It's impossible if you want it to use the index.

Perhaps you can use dynamic SQL (EXECUTE IMMEDIATE).

☞ QUESTION 15

SQL Query not using Composite Index

Please look at the query below:

```
SELECT pde.participant_uid
,pde.award_code
,pde.award_type
,SUM(decode(pde.distribution_type
,'FORFEITURE'
,pde.forfeited_quantity *
pde.sold_price * cc.rate
,pde.distributed_quantity *
pde.sold_price * cc.rate)) AS gross_Amt_pref_Curr
FROM part_distribution_exec pde
,currency_conversion cc
,currency off_curr
WHERE pde.participant_uid = 4105
AND off_curr.currency_iso_code =
pde.offering_currency_iso_code
AND cc.from_currency_uid = off_curr.currency_uid
AND cc.to_currency_uid = 1
AND cc.latest_flag = 'Y'
GROUP BY pde.participant_uid
,pde.award_code
,pde.award_type
```

In oracle 9i, I've executed the above query. It took 6 seconds and the cost was 616, and this is because of not using the composite index.

"Currency_conversion_idx(From_currency_uid,   To_currency_uid, Latest_flag)".

Is there a reason why this index was not used while executing the above query? I dropped the index and recreated it. Now, the query is using this index. After inserting many rows even after a day, the same query was executed but the query did not use the index again. So everyday, the index should be dropped and recreated.

Is there a solution for this?

✍ ANSWER

The issue might be due to the following possibilities:

1. The CBO doesn't get the latest stats (assuming you don't have "optimiser_mode=rule")

   You can address this by collecting stats using "DBMS_ STATS", (Oracle suggested) or analyze for the table/index involved possibly every night.

2. The selectivity of the index is poor. I.e. number of rows per distinct key is high, hence, sometimes CBO thinks it is better not to use index.

   You can address this partially, by passing hint to use the appropriate index if you are sure that selectivity is not really poor, and you will benefit using that index. Although, not using the index is not a bad thing all the time.

☞ QUESTION 16

Query takes a lot of time to execute

I have one query, which takes 7-8 minutes to execute.

The query is based on 4 tables.

The table "IBS_WORK_BANKDATA" contains 120000 records,
"IBS_ORG_BANKDATA" contains 110000 records,
"IBS_CURRENCYMASTER" contains 178 records, and
"IBS_CURRENCYEXCHANGEMASTER" contains 58 records.

Query:

select distinct trim(wrk.bd_alcd) as ALCD, wrk.bd_typecd as TypeCD, wrk.bd_forcd as FORCD, wrk.bd_curcd as CURCD,
   wrk.bd_councd as COUNCD, wrk.bd_sectcd as SECCD,
   wrk.bd_matcd as MATCD, wrk.bd_c_u_cd as C_U_CD,
   wrk.bd_s_u_cd as S_U_CD,
   0 as Org_FCBal,0 as ORG_Bal,case when wrk.bd_type='O' then wrk.bd_fc_bal else 0 end as Main_FCBal,
   case when wrk.bd_type='O' then (wrk.bd_fc_bal * nvl(exchg.cer_exchangerate, 1)) else 0 end as main_Bal,
   wrk.bd_rs_int,wrk.bd_rs_bal,wrk.bd_fc_int,wrk.bd_fc_bal,
   ' ' as TrackChangs
   from ibs_work_bankdata wrk inner join ibs_org_bankdata org ON org.bd_yrqtr = wrk.bd_yrqtr and org.bd_bkcode=wrk.bd_bkcode and org.bd_forcd = wrk.bd_forcd

and wrk.BD_YRQTR=20044 and wrk.BD_BKCODE
='000'
and wrk.BD_ALCD = '51' and wrk.BD_FORCD ='IN' and
wrk.BD_TYPECD = '11'
left join ibs_currencymaster curmst on curmst.cur_code =
wrk.bd_curcd
left join ibs_currencyexchangerate exchg on exchg.cer_
currencyid = curmst.cur_id
and exchg.cer_yearqtr = 20051 and exchg.CER_ACTIVE=1
union select distinct trim(wrk.bd_alcd) as ALCD, wrk.
bd_typecd as TypeCD, wrk.bd_forcd as FORCD, wrk.
bd_curcd as CURCD,
wrk.bd_councd as COUNCD, wrk.bd_sectcd as SECCD,
wrk.bd_matcd as MATCD, ' ' as C_U_CD, ' ' as S_U_CD,
0 as Org_FCBal,0 as ORG_Bal,case when wrk.bd_type='O'
then wrk.bd_fc_bal else 0 end as Main_FCBal,
case when wrk.bd_type='O' then (wrk.bd_fc_bal *
nvl(exchg.cer_exchangerate, 1)) else 0 end as main_Bal,
wrk.bd_rs_int,wrk.bd_rs_bal,wrk.bd_fc_int,wrk.bd_fc_
bal,
' ' as TrackChangs
from ibs_work_bankdata wrk inner join ibs_org_bankdata
org ON org.bd_yrqtr = wrk.bd_yrqtr and org.bd_bkcode=wrk.
bd_bkcode and org.bd_forcd = wrk.bd_forcd
and wrk.BD_YRQTR=20044 and wrk.BD_BKCODE
='000'
and wrk.BD_ALCD = '51' and wrk.BD_FORCD ='IN' and
wrk.BD_TYPECD = '11' and wrk.bd_rs_bal>0
left join ibs_currencymaster curmst on curmst.cur_code =
wrk.bd_curcd
left join ibs_currencyexchangerate exchg on exchg.cer_
currencyid = curmst.cur_id
and exchg.cer_yearqtr = 20051 and exchg.CER_ACTIVE=1
order by main_FCBal

Explain_plan:
SELECT STATEMENT, GOAL = CHOOSE   Cost=429
Cardinality=2 Bytes=314
SORT UNIQUE   Cost=402   Cardinality=2
Bytes=314
UNION-ALL
TABLE ACCESS BY INDEX ROWID   Object owner=RBI
Object name=IBS_ORG_BANKDATA Cost=54
Cardinality=204   Bytes=2856
NESTED LOOPS   Cost=174   Cardinality=41
Bytes=6437
NESTED LOOPS OUTER   Cost=120   Cardinality=1
Bytes=143
 NESTED LOOPS OUTER   Cost=119   Cardinality=1
Bytes=93
TABLE ACCESS BY INDEX ROWID   Object owner=RBI
Object name=IBS_WORK_BANKDATA   Cost=118
Cardinality=1 Bytes=52
INDEX SKIP SCAN   Object owner=RBI   O b j e c t
name=IBS_WORK_BANKDATA_IDX   Cost=59
Cardinality=1
TABLE ACCESS BY INDEX ROWID   Object owner=RBI
Object name=IBS_CURRENCYMASTER   Cost=1
Cardinality=178   Bytes=7298
INDEX RANGE SCAN Object owner=RBI
Object name=IBS_CURRENCYMASTER_CODE
Cardinality=178
TABLE ACCESS BY INDEX ROWID   Object owner=RBI
Object name=IBS_CURRENCYEXCHANGERATE   Cost=1
Cardinality=19 Bytes=950
INDEX RANGE SCAN Object owner=RBI   O b j e c t
name=IBS_CURRENCYEXCH_CURRENCYID
Cardinality=19
INDEX RANGE SCAN Object owner=RBI   O b j e c t
name=IBS_ORG_BANKDATA_IDX   Cost=19

Cardinality=204
TABLE ACCESS BY INDEX ROWID Object owner=RBI
Object name=IBS_ORG_BANKDATA   Cost=54
Cardinality=204   Bytes=2856
NESTED LOOPS   Cost=174   Cardinality=41
Bytes=6437
NESTED LOOPS OUTER   Cost=120   Cardinality=1
Bytes=143
NESTED LOOPS OUTER   Cost=119   Cardinality=1
Bytes=93
TABLE ACCESS BY INDEX ROWID Object owner=RBI
Object name=IBS_WORK_BANKDATA   Cost=118
Cardinality=1 Bytes=52
INDEX SKIP SCAN   Object owner=RBI   O b j e c t
name=IBS_WORK_BANKDATA_IDX Cost=59
Cardinality=1
TABLE ACCESS BY INDEX ROWID Object owner=RBI
Object name=IBS_CURRENCYMASTER   Cost=1
Cardinality=178   Bytes=7298
INDEX RANGE SCAN Object owner=RBI
Object name=IBS_CURRENCYMASTER_CODE
Cardinality=178
TABLE ACCESS BY INDEX ROWID Object owner=RBI
Object name=IBS_CURRENCYEXCHANGERATE   Cost=1
Cardinality=19   Bytes=950
INDEX RANGE SCAN Object owner=RBI   O b j e c t
name=IBS_CURRENCYEXCH_CURRENCYID
Cardinality=19
INDEX RANGE SCAN Object owner=RBI   O b j e c t
name=IBS_ORG_BANKDATA_IDX   Cost=19
Cardinality=204

How do I find the solution for this?

✍ ANSWER

To increase your query performance, you have to build a materialized view on it. So every time you execute the query, the optimizer will access the materialized view table, and get the data from it. Once you create the materialized view optimizer, access the four tables once. Make the necessary join instead of accessing the four tables. Hash joins every time you issue the query.

```
-set QUERY_REWRITE_ENABLED to TRUE.
-CREATE MATERIALIZED VIEW anyname
ENABLE QUERY REWRITE
AS
select distinct trim(wrk.bd_alcd) as ALCD, wrk.bd_typecd
as TypeCD, wrk.bd_forcd as FORCD, wrk.bd_curcd as
CURCD,
wrk.bd_councd as COUNCD, wrk.bd_sectcd as SECCD,
wrk.bd_matcd as MATCD, wrk.bd_c_u_cd as C_U_CD, wrk.
bd_s_u_cd as S_U_CD,
0 as Org_FCBal,0 as ORG_Bal,case when wrk.bd_type='O'
then wrk.bd_fc_bal else 0 end as Main_FCBal,
case when wrk.bd_type='O' then (wrk.bd_fc_bal * nvl(exchg.
cer_exchangerate, 1)) else 0 end as main_Bal,
wrk.bd_rs_int,wrk.bd_rs_bal,wrk.bd_fc_int,wrk.bd_fc_bal,
' ' as TrackChangs
from ibs_work_bankdata wrk inner join ibs_org_bankdata
org ON org.bd_yrqtr = wrk.bd_yrqtr and org.bd_bkcode=wrk.
bd_bkcode and org.bd_forcd = wrk.bd_forcd
and wrk.BD_YRQTR=20044 and wrk.BD_BKCODE ='000'
and wrk.BD_ALCD = '51' and wrk.BD_FORCD ='IN' and wrk.
BD_TYPECD = '11'
left join ibs_currencymaster curmst on curmst.cur_code =
```

wrk.bd_curcd

left join ibs_currencyexchangerate exchg on exchg.cer_
currencyid = curmst.cur_id

and exchg.cer_yearqtr = 20051 and exchg.CER_ACTIVE=1
union select distinct trim(wrk.bd_alcd) as ALCD, wrk.bd_
typecd as TypeCD, wrk.bd_forcd as FORCD, wrk.bd_curcd
as CURCD,

wrk.bd_councd as COUNCD, wrk.bd_sectcd as SECCD,
wrk.bd_matcd as MATCD, ' ' as C_U_CD, ' ' as S_U_CD,

0 as Org_FCBal,0 as ORG_Bal,case when wrk.bd_type='O'
then wrk.bd_fc_bal else 0 end as Main_FCBal,

case when wrk.bd_type='O' then (wrk.bd_fc_bal * nvl(exchg.
cer_exchangerate, 1)) else 0 end as main_Bal,

wrk.bd_rs_int,wrk.bd_rs_bal,wrk.bd_fc_int,wrk.bd_fc_bal,
' ' as TrackChangs

from ibs_work_bankdata wrk inner join ibs_org_bankdata
org ON org.bd_yrqtr = wrk.bd_yrqtr and org.bd_bkcode=wrk.
bd_bkcode and org.bd_forcd = wrk.bd_forcd

and wrk.BD_YRQTR=20044 and wrk.BD_BKCODE ='000'
and wrk.BD_ALCD = '51' and wrk.BD_FORCD ='IN' and wrk.
BD_TYPECD = '11' and wrk.bd_rs_bal>0

left join ibs_currencymaster curmst on curmst.cur_code =
wrk.bd_curcd

left join ibs_currencyexchangerate exchg on exchg.cer_
currencyid = curmst.cur_id

and exchg.cer_yearqtr = 20051 and exchg.CER_ACTIVE=1
order by main_FCBal;

☞ QUESTION 17

Bad view and slow reports

I have an old and bad set up, with a bunch of reports, which runs off regular views. With the table growth, the reports are running slower. I cannot change the reports; they will run the way they are now for at least for 2-3 months until the development team puts the new one on production. I suggested replacing the views with Materialized views, which saved us a lot of time in the past. The management did not agree. What else can I do to improve the views? Here is one of them:

```
CREATE VIEW DATA1 AS
select '1' as ord, s.test_id, s. ent1 as ent_id, 'Name' as data_type,
n.last_name || ', ' || n.first_name || ' ' || n.mid_name || ' ' || n.name_gen as data_value
from name n, s_con s
where s.conf_ent1 = n.ent_id
union
select '2' as ord, s.s_test_id, s.conf_ent1 as ent_id, 'Address' as data_type,
a.addr1 || ' ' || addr2 || ' ' || addr3 || ' ' || city || ' ' || state_code || ' ' || country_code as data_value
from s_con s, address a
where s.conf_ent1 = a.ent_id
union
select '3' as ord, s.s_test_id, s.conf_ent1 as ent_id,
(select t.num_desc from num_type t where n.num_type_id = t.num_type_id) as data_type, n.num_value as data_value
from s_con s, nums n
```

where s.conf_ent1 = n.ent_id
union
select '5' as ord, s.s_test_id, s.conf_ent1 as ent_id,
'Email' as data_type,e.email as data_value
from s_con s, emaile
where s.conf_ent1 = e.ent_id;

It uses the indexes on the name, address, e-mail tables, but
always does a "FTS" on "s_con" as it selects almost all of the
table.

✍ ANSWER

The only real improvement I could suggest (other than
designing the data model from scratch) is to use "UNION
ALL", instead of "UNION".

```
CREATE OR REPLACE VIEW data1
(ord
,  test_id
,  ent_id
,  data_type
,  data_value)
AS
SELECT  x.ord
,     s.test_id
,     DECODE(x.ord
      ,   '1', s.ent1
      ,   x.ent_id)              ent_id
,     x.data_type
,     x.data_value
FROM  (SELECT '1'                ord
      ,   n.ent_id               ent_id
      ,   'Name'                 data_type
```

```
  ,     n.last_name
        || ', '
        || n.first_name
        || DECODE(n.mid_name
        ,     NULL, NULL
        ,     ' ' || n.mid_name)
        || DECODE(n.name_gen
        ,     NULL, NULL
        ,     ' ' || n.name_gen)    data_value
  FROM  name            n
  UNION ALL
  SELECT '2'                    ord
  ,     a.ent_id          ent_id
  ,     'Address'         data_type
  ,     a.addr1
        || DECODE(a.addr2
        ,     NULL, NULL
        ,     a.addr2 || ' ')
        || DECODE(a.addr3
        ,     NULL, NULL
        ,     a.addr3 || ' ')
        || a.city
        || ' '
        || a.state_code
        || DECODE(a.country_code
        ,     NULL, NULL
        ,     ' ' || a.country_code) data_value
  FROM  address          a
  UNION ALL
  SELECT '3'                    ord
  ,     nu.ent_id         ent_id
  ,     t.num_desc        data_type
  ,     nu.num_value            data_value
  FROM  nums             nu
  ,     num_type         t
```

```
      WHERE  nu.num_type_id = t.num_type_id
      UNION ALL
      SELECT '5'                    ord
      ,    e.ent_id               ent_id
      ,    'Email'                data_type
      ,    e.email                data_value
      FROM   email          e) x
,    s_con               s
WHERE   s.conf_ent1 = x.ent_id
```

The full table scan on "S_CON" is understandable. Remember, just because it's a full table scan, it doesn't mean it's bad.

☞ QUESTION **18**

Statistics, to update or not

It's taught that every time we have a change in the data, we need to update object statistics. Most of the time, the table with "Cascade option = true for all index columns". I have "OLTP - 1000 trxs/sec average", which is a huge insert rate. I used to update my stats after every big load of data nightly, with an average of 6 million rows inserted. When I have to set up a new test environment, I run the application for a while to get enough data, and then run "dbms_stats" to gather the stats.

The same type of application runs on DB2. The DB2 guys are using a different approach. They collect statistics from a test environment, and import them into the new database. Since they are sure that they have the right execution plans, they completely disabled all auto update stats options, and never run statistics again. The presumption is that, if once we have the right execution plans, nothing should ever change in the statistics.

They want me to apply the same approach for Oracle. I think that when I insert with crazy speed, I would need to update the statistics to give the optimizer more info for the new structures.

Any thoughts on how the Db2 approach will reflect Oracle performance?

✍ ANSWER

When you recalculate your statistics and there's no change, there is no need to analyze. Analyze is worthless if your plans don't change. The DB2 guy's approach is valid. Provided you are happy with the plans exactly as they are, and you know your data well enough that you can't foresee future "insert/update/delete" patterns that would run poorly under these plans, then it's fine.

The only consideration I can see is with time-sensitive histograms. Consider the SQL.

```
SELECT *
FROM big_table
WHERE insert_date > SYSDATE - 10
```

With up to date statistics, Oracle could use its histograms to determine that there are few rows matching this query, and you should use an index to retrieve them. Without this knowledge, the "default" plan may be a full table scan.

If this sort of thing is important in your system, then stick with your current approach.

☞ QUESTION **19**

Tuning: Multiple table inner join query with partitioning

I have a query that is quite bulky. The query is used in a partition by selection statement (for summation). It is then joined with another set from those same tables, which meets the same criteria (it can't be included in first select because of different groupings). I need to optimize this because it runs very slow. It would make sense to hint some ordering in the inner joins, given the way the data was organized. However, I can't seem to convince the optimizer to do anything else than left to right.

Here is the select statement, without the partition:

```
SELECT <Fields>
FROM hist
INNER JOIN stat USING (k1)
INNER JOIN cl_art ON stat.k2=cl_art.k2
INNER JOIN cl_loc USING (k3)
INNER JOIN loc ON loc.k4=cl_loc.k4
INNER JOIN sale ON sale.k4 = loc.k4
AND sale.k2 = stat.k2
WHERE sale.<has 3 restrictions>
AND stat.<has 2 restrictions>
AND hist.<has 1 restriction>
AND cl_art.(has 4 restrictions>
AND cl_loc.<has 4 restrictions>
AND loc.<has 2 restrictions>
```

Now with "ANSI JOINS", it is said you can use parentheses

to indicate ordering. Here I run into two issues:

- I can't get it to work
- the optimizer decides what path to follow by it self, no matter how many parentheses you place.

Ideally, I would want to do the following:

> inner join hist with stat with cl_art.
> inner join cl_loc with loc.
> inner join those two subsets.
> inner join this subset with sale.

At least, I assume inner join is the best option. Of all tables, >60% will be used except from the sale table, of which about .1% will be used (it's HUGE but partitioned usefully by date).

Using parentheses, it would look like this:

```
SELECT <Fields> FROM
(((((hist
INNER JOIN stat USING (k1))
INNER JOIN cl_art ON stat.k2=cl_art.k2)
INNER JOIN cl_loc USING (k3)
(INNER JOIN loc ON loc.k4=cl_loc.k4))
INNER JOIN sale ON sale.k4 = loc.k4 AND sale.k2 =
stat.k2)
WHERE ...
```

It doesn't work, am I missing the right parenthesis on the 6th line?

Is it true that I am loosing a lot of time on parsing so I should hint "/*+ordered*/, optimizer_search_limit"? Is there another way to optimize?

✍ Answer

In most of the cases you should NOT use hints. These days, you should work with CBO and have stats on your tables and indexes. The optimizer will choose for the most appropriate execution plan. Hints are often used despite the exceptions. You can format your trace files with "tkprof".

WHERE sale.<has 3 restrictions>
AND stat.<has 2 restrictions>
AND hist.<has 1 restriction>
AND cl_art.(has 4 restrictions>
AND cl_loc.<has 4 restrictions>
AND loc.<has 2 restrictions>

You may want to use composite indexes for the multi-restriction.

Where exists in: "(not)exists operator" or "(not)in operator"

If you want play with hints, this one will process the from list from left to right

SQL> select /*+ ORDERED USE_MERGE (a,b,c) */ a.col1,a.col2,b.col1,b.col2,c.col1,c.col2 from t1 a,t2 b,t3 c where ...
SQL> select /*+ ORDERED USE_NL (a,b,c) */ a.col1,a.col2,b.col1,b.col2,c.col1,c.col2 from t1 a,t2 b,t3 c where ...
SQL> select /*+ ORDERED USE_HASH (a,b,c) */ a.col1,a.col2,b.col1,b.col2,c.col1,c.col2 from t1 a,t2 b,t3 c where ...

You can also look at Oracle SQL*Plus Pocket Reference by O'Reily, 1.3.5.3.

The Join Order is when joining more than two tables, use parentheses to control the join order. If you omit parentheses, Oracle processes the joins from left to right.

☞ QUESTION 20

Shrinking index table space

I'm using Oracle 8i. The data files were full before, but the indexes were moved to a different tablespace. This left a lot of scattered space in the tablespace.

If I move some indexes from the index tablespace to another tablespace, how can I claim the free size of the previous index tablespace? How can I shrink the previous tablespace?

✍ ANSWER

Just check if you can coalesce a table space.

Syntax:

    SQL> alter tablespace HRINDEX coalesce;

In addition, if you are using 10g version of the oracle and ASSM, you can search for "ALTER INDEX <INDEX_NAME> SHRINK SPACE;".

If 9/8 version, then search for: "ALTER DATABASE DATAFILE '/full path/datafile.dbf' RESIZE size XX[K|M];". This will help only if the last extent was never used.

☞ QUESTION 21

Turn logging on, on Index

I rebuild an index, "alter index owner.index_name rebuild tablespace tablespace_name parallel 4 nologging;".

Is this the correct syntax? If it is, how do I turn the logging back on?

✍ ANSWER

The syntax is correct. This is the output:

SQL> alter index PK_EMP_EMPNO rebuild tablespace USERDATA parallel 4 nologging;

Index altered.

To enable logging, do the following:

SQL> alter index PK_EMP_EMPNO rebuild tablespace USERDATA parallel 4 logging;

Index altered.

######### OR ##########

SQL> alter index PK_EMP_EMPNO rebuild tablespace USERDATA parallel 4;

Index altered.

☞ **QUESTION 22**

change snapshot timing

I started to run the snapshot in order to generate the stats pack report. By default it was set to one hour. How can I change the time in order to take snapshot within a period of 3 minutes?

✍ **ANSWER**

Create a "dbms" job with an interval of 3 minutes.

> 'SYSDATE + 3/1440'

Then, put the following in the 'what' condition ..

> statspack.snap;

☞ QUESTION 23

Query, using bind variable is slower

My user complains querying the DB using bind variable,
because it is slower than using SQL-Plus. He suggested to
remove the bind variables from the DB cache.

How can I explain that using bind variable makes the query
slow?

The user sent me 2 of his queries:

    SELECT COUNT(DISTINCT t0.POLID)
    FROM POLSEA t1, POLRES t0
    WHERE (t0.POLID = t1.ENTID
    AND t1.ENTTYP = :1
    AND t1.POLNO LIKE :2)

and

    SELECT   DISTINCT   t0.POLID,   t0.CLASS,   t0.LOCK,
    t0.ACCTID, t0.BTYP, t0.ACODE, t0.ANAME, t0.CDATE,
    t0.CNAME, t0.CNO, t0.EDATE, t0.EXDATE, t0.ADDR,
    t0.SX, t0.INAME, t0.LDATE, t0.PERF, t0.POLENG,
    t0.POLNO, t0.PRD, t0.STT, t0.UCO, t0.UCX
    FROM POLSEA t1, POLRES t0
    WHERE (t0.POLID = t1.ENTID
    AND t1.ENTTYP = :1
    AND t1.POLNO LIKE :2)

✍ ANSWER

You can get comparative explain plan's for with, and without bind variables. Doubtless, Oracle is using its knowledge of the data distribution to choose a better plan when constant values are used. Constant value predicates and allows the optimizer to choose the best possible plan for those values. If three different sets of values result in three separate optimal plans, (optimal for that combination of values) then constant predicates handles that, but bind variables won"t.

With bind variables, Oracle must choose one execution plan only to cover all possible combinations of bind values. Some will be optimal, some won't.

The reason bind variables are encouraged, is not because they result in more optimal SQL, but because they don't clog up the shared pool with many versions of the same SQL.

If the SQL is part of the user-accessible front-end, you must use bind variables. You can't have thousands of 'identical' SQL's in the shared pool because you'll bring the database to its knees.

☞ QUESTION **24**

SQL with a very slow response

I'm using the following query based on 3 tables:

mem has 2 million,
act has 17 million and
trx has 27 million records

SELECT
MEM.MEMHIP_NO,
ACT.ACTIVITY_DATE,
TRX.TRANSACTION_DATE,
TRX.trx_fact,
.....
FROM
MEM,
ACT,
TRX
WHERE
(ACT.MEMBER_ACTIVITY_ID(+)=TRX.MEMBER_
ACTIVITY_ID)
AND (MEM.MEMBER_ID=TRX.MEMBER_ID)
AND (TRX.USER_CREATED = ????)
AND TRX.TRx_DATE BETWEEN '1-Jan-2005' AND '31-
DEC-2005'
AND
.... some other conditions....)

This query runs very slow. It takes 4-5 hours to refresh the
data. All indexes and joins are accurate and I'm also using
normal as well as BIT map indexes. Before, I also used hints.

- 47 -

In some cases it helped, but not all the time.

How can I improve the performance and tune this query?

✍ ANSWER

You can fix this by setting the undocumented "initSID.ora parameter

_make_query_faster=TRUE".

☞ QUESTION 25

Tablespace increase

We have SAP R/3 4.7 Enterprise edition. Oracle 8.1.7.4.0 database, and Operating System Redhat Linux 2.4.9.

We increase our tablespace PSAPPML by 1 data file every 10 days, once it reaches 99%. 1 data file size is 2 GB. Is it a optimal increase?

The problem is, PSAPPML tablespace soon reaches 99% using our present scenario. Presently our oracle mount point is:

Mount Point : /oracle
Allocated : 255 GB
Free : 86 GB

Which is the best method to increase 1 data file every week, or to increase bulk data file? Should we increase 2 or 3 data files at a time, once every month?

✍ ANSWER

It may or may not increase because it depends on your "Backup/OS limit/oracle" configurations. On a given time, you will hit the wall (reaching maxdatafiles/db_files). You can just extend your datafile (instead of adding a new one), but your backup/ recovery options should be considered.

Tablespace can increase 2g within a week (Unless you really load 2G worth data with the timeframe).

If you are in DMT, try to migrate to LMT (preferably to 10g/9i). If this is the case, you have to live with DMT. Make sure you have tablespaces/objects defined as "INITIAL=NEXT" and "PCTINCREASE=0".

If you happen to do massive deletes/inserts, maybe the tables need the HWM to reset. You should also coalesce the tablespace. Make sure you do preventive maintenance such as a regular or scheduled online rebuild of indexes.

☞ QUESTION 26

Explain Plan

I have a table dept as follows:

> Dept(Table) Total Rows:-1000
> Deptno (primary Key)
> Description (non unique index)

I fire a Query:

> explain plan for select * from dept
> where deptno=10 or description ='Description-1'

and the explain plan generated was:

> SELECT STATEMENT CHOOSE
> TABLE ACCESS DEPT FULL

Why is the table scan not concatenated? Is it because of using
Multiple or contained indexed columns?

✍ ANSWER

There are many factors why your index was not used. You
should check if you collected the statistics or indexes.
Another reason might be because of your "OR" ">>or
description = 'Description-1". You can analyze the table dept
compute statistics, and explain plan for select "* from dept
where deptno=10;".

The query is involving multiple, or with different indexed columns. It should use concatenation. All the tables and indexes are already analyzed or statistics are computed.

It depends on the actual data distribution and available statistics to the CBO.

Based on the available statistics, CBO will decide the plan.

I took the regular emp table here.

```
scott@9i > get emp_loopinsert;
1  begin
2  for mag in 1..15 loop
3      insert into emp (select * from emp);
4  end loop;
5  commit;
 6* end;
scott@9i > @emp_loopinsert
```

PL/SQL procedure successfully completed.

```
scott@9i > select count(*) from emp;
```

COUNT(*)

 458752

```
scott@9i > create index deptno_index on
emp(deptno);
```

Index created.

```
scott@9i > create index job_index on emp(job);
Index created.
```

```
scott@9i > analyze table emp compute statistics for
all indexed columns;
```

Table analyzed.

scott@9i > set autotrace traceonly exp
scott@9i > select ename from emp where job=
'CLERK' or DEPTNO=10;

Execution Plan

----

    0   SELECT STATEMENT Optimizer=CHOOSE
    1   0   CONCATENATION
    2   1   TABLE ACCESS (BY INDEX ROWID) OF
'EMP'
    3   2   INDEX (RANGE SCAN) OF 'DEPTNO_
INDEX' (NON-UNIQUE)
    4   1   TABLE ACCESS (BY INDEX ROWID) OF
'EMP'
    5   4   INDEX (RANGE SCAN) OF 'JOB_INDEX'
(NON-UNIQUE)

scott@9i > exec dbms_stats.set_table_stats('SCOTT
','EMP',NUMROWS=>100);

PL/SQL procedure successfully completed.

scott@9i > select ename from emp where job='CLERK'
or DEPTNO=10;

Execution Plan

----

    0   SELECT STATEMENT Optimizer=CHOOSE
(Cost=11 Card=44 Bytes=704
)

1   0   TABLE ACCESS (FULL) OF 'EMP' (Cost=11 Card=44
Bytes=704)

☞ QUESTION 27

Tuning this query

Can anyone help me to TUNE the query below? The cost of query is 55000+. When I add the condition "pnd.packing_notes_id = 16985549", the cost is less, i.e. 48. Proper index exist in Primary Key & Foreign Keys.

```
SELECT count(1) A
FROM
logistics.arrival_groups ag,
dispatch_labels dl,
dispatch_note_details dd,
styles s,
style_colls sc,
sysmodule.companies comp,
sysmodule.departments d,
orders o,
customer_groups cg2,
order_details od,
logistics.packing_note_details pnd,
customer_groups cg,
temp_distributions td,
logistics.transport_advis ta,
arrivals ar

WHERE
ag.arrival_groups_id = ar.arrival_groups_id
-----------------------------------------------------------------------
AND (dl.status = 'PRINTED' OR dd.purchase_no IS
NULL)
AND dl.dispatch_notes_id(+) = dd.dispatch_notes_id
AND dd.purchase_no(+) = o.order_number
```

AND s.deleted = 'N'
AND s.styles_id = sc.styles_id
AND sc.style_colls_id = o.style_colls_id
AND comp.deleted = 'N'
AND comp.companies_id = o.companies_id_2

AND d.deleted = 'N'
AND d.departments_id = o.departments_id

AND o.deleted = 'N'
AND o.orders_id = od.orders_id

AND cg2.deleted = 'N'
AND cg2.customer_groups_id = od.customer_groups_id
AND od.order_details_id = pnd.order_details_id

–AND pnd.packing_notes_id = 16985549
AND pnd.packing_note_details_id = ta.packing_note_
details_id

–AND cg.group_name = 'NORWAY'
–AND ((:P_CUSTOMERGROUPS_ID is null) or (upper(:
P_CUSTOMERGROUPS_ID)
– = upper(cg.GROUP_NAME)))
AND cg.deleted = 'N'
AND (cg.customer_groups_id = td.customer_groups_id
OR cg.customer_groups_id = od.customer_groups_id)

AND td.packing_note_details_id(+) = ta.packing_note_
details_id

AND ta.deleted = 'N'
AND ta.transport_advis_id = ar.transport_advis_id

AND ar.arrival_date BETWEEN '01-JUN-2005' AND '31-DEC-2005'

GROUP BY
cg.group_name,
ar.arrival_date,
o.order_number,
d.department_name,
s.style_name,
s.style_number,
od.customer_groups_id,
cg2.group_name,
ta.order_number,
od.order_details_id,
od.line_number,
cg.customer_groups_id,
dl.TO_NUMBER,
dl.from_number,
pnd.packing_notes_id

The following tables are accessed fully by the query:

transport_advis
order_details
packing_note_details
departments
orders
companies

✎ ANSWER

Try to use the plan table to see what the optimizer is trying to do.

Try indexing each table with the columns in the same order that you used in the 'where' part of the query. I.e. if you said in your where clause 'where ag.arrival_groups_id = ar.arrival_groups_id', then put an index on ag and ar that have "arrival_groups_id" in it, as the first segment of that index.

Avoid full table scans if the cardinality of the table is large. Some where clauses have functions in them that increase the likelihood of full table scans, such as the 'nval' function.

Put the data and the indexes in tablespaces that live on separate disks. (i.e. data_01 tablespace using a datafile on "/u01 and indx_02" tablespace with a datafile on "/u02", or windows, data on D drive, and the indexes on E drive)

You have a lot of group in your query. Try to check if you can do that in memory rather than on disk. If you have the physical memory, you can increase the parameter "sort_area_size" in some versions.

Check to see that you have enough physical memory to support your sga, pga, and processes (no swapping).

Start with a less restrictive where clause, and add to the where clause until you find the one(s) that makes it slow.

If everything fails, try to break the query into pieces by using 'pl/sql' or 3rd party software with api's. You would create a collection using a query, and fetch though the collection eliminating rows based on your where clause.

Make sure your query is correct first, (returns the correct result set) before worrying about it running faster.

☞ QUESTION **28**

The difference between 2 execution method

When I am calling the "schedule_util.get_resource_blocks_
schedule" table function through a select statement, it is
taking less than a second to execute.

But when I am calling "schedule_util.get_schedules
procedure" through "procedure test_get_schedules", which
in turn calls "schedule_util.get_resource_blocks_schedule"
table function, execution time is nearly 10 secs.

Can somebody tell me how to improve the performance
using the wrapper procedure?
Here are the required procedures and functions given:

```
select *
from table(
schedule_util.get_resource_blocks_schedule(
null,
equipment_array('CT ROOM1'),
to_date('11/04/2005 09:00', 'MM/DD/RRRR HH24:MI'),
to_date('11/04/2006 09:00', 'MM/DD/RRRR HH24:MI'),
'forwards',
'OP',
'available',
null,
null,
'byTime'
)
) where rownum <= 10
/
```

The above statement took less than a second.

```
CREATE OR REPLACE procedure test_get_schedules
(
out_resource_blocks out sys_refcursor
)
as
begin
schedule_util.get_schedules
(
null, -- in_org_obj_aguid
'01FA409FDE1A4BB4A71E526343B30DFD',    --    in_
equipment_obj_aguid
'11/10/2005 05:00', -- in_start_dt
null, -- in_end_dt
'forwards',    --    in_date_direction    ('forwards'    or
'backwards')
'OP', -- in_patient_type
'available', -- in_category -- null, Available, or Unavailable
null, -- in_procedure_aguid
null, -- in_duration -- in minutes (overrides equip.duration
& proc.duration)
'byTime', -- in_layout_style
3, -- in_max_rowcount
out_resource_blocks -- sys_refcursor returning data
);

end;
/
```

This took nearly 10 seconds.

Here is the "schedule_util.get_schedules" procedure:

```
procedure get_schedules(
```

```
in_org_obj_aguid in equipment_t.org_obj_aguid%type
,in_equipment_obj_aguid in equipment_t.obj_aguid%type
,in_start_date in varchar2
,in_end_date in varchar2
,in_date_direction in varchar2
,in_patient_type      in      top_proc_dates_t.patient_type_
code%type
,in_category in varchar2 -- null, Available, or Unavailable
,in_procedure_aguid in procedure_t.obj_aguid%type
,in_duration in pls_integer – in minutes
,in_layout_style in varchar2 -- subsort beneath byDay;
valid    values:    constants.kScheduleLayoutByTime    or
constants.kScheduleLayoutByEquipment, see Constants
,in_max_rowcount in pls_integer
,out_resource_blocks out sys_refcursor
) is
the_equipments equipment_array := null;
the_date_direction varchar2(255);
the_start_date date;
the_end_date date;
the_tmp_date date;
begin
if(in_equipment_obj_aguid is not null) then
the_equipments := equipment_array(in_equipment_obj_
aguid);
end if;

-- initialize date range to non-null values
the_start_date := to_date(in_start_date, 'MM/DD/RRRR
HH24:MI');
the_end_date := to_date(in_end_date, 'MM/DD/RRRR
HH24:MI');
if(the_start_date is null) then
the_start_date := sysdate;
end if;
```

```
if(the_end_date is null) then
the_end_date := the_start_date + 365;
end if;

open out_resource_blocks
for select
resource_obj_aguid
,start_date
,start_time
,end_time
,status
from     table(get_resource_blocks_schedule(in_org_obj_
aguid
,the_equipments
,the_start_date
,the_end_date
,in_date_direction
,in_patient_type
,in_category
,in_procedure_aguid
,in_duration
,in_layout_style)) x
where (in_max_rowcount <= 0 or rownum <= in_max_
rowcount);
end get_schedules;
```

✍ ANSWER

"ALTER SESSION SET SQLTRACE = TRUE;"
Run something like this: "ALTER SESSION SET SQLTRACE
= FALSE;"
Do the same thing for both executions in separate sessions,
and use 'TK*Prof' to analyze the results. The difference
should be fairly obvious from the 'tk_prof' output.

☞ QUESTION **29**

Why AWR doesn't collect statistics information

Is there a solution for this?

```
<?php
SQL> show parameter statistics

NAME                          TYPE      VALUE
----------------------------- --------- -------------------
statistics_level              string    TYPICAL
timed_os_statistics           integer   0
timed_statistics              boolean   TRUE

SQL> select count(*) from DBA_HIST_SNAPSHOT;

  COUNT(*)
---------
        0

Elapsed: 00:00:00.00
SQL>
?>
```

✍ **ANSWER**

The default snapshot interval is 1 hour. Wait after 1 hour then try again.

If it doesn't help, check your interval:

SQL> SELECT snap_interval FROM dba_hist_wr_
control;

SNAP_INTERVAL

+00000 01:00:00.0

☞ QUESTION 30

Issue in temporary tablespace

We have Oracle 8.1.7.0 as our database. We used dictionary
managed temporary tablespace. Now, I created a new locally
managed temporary tablespace, and assigned that tablespace to
all of the users. The space usage in DMT should be 0, but it
showed 157 Mb since the day when I transferred the users from
DMT to LMT. Why this is so?

✍ ANSWER

Query the dictionary to see what objects are in that
tablespace:

    SELECT   segment_type,   owner,   segment_name
FROM dba_extents

    WHERE tablespace_name = 'OLD_TEMP_TS'

☞ **QUESTION 31**

force a hash join

Does anybody know if and how I can force Oracle to do hash
outer join to an inline view? I know that every row in the
both tables contained in the view will be hit. Theoretically,
it should be faster to do a full table scan with hash join. But
I can't seem to get Oracle to do it so I can test it. I tried the
"USE_HASH" hint as shown below. I tried a FULL hint on the
tables in view. Is there a hindrance in the oracle that I'm not
aware of?

```
SELECT   /*+ORDERED  FULL(a)  PARALLEL(a)  FULL(b)
PARALLEL(b)USE_HASH(a fim)*/
    a.record_seq_num,
    a.cusip,
    a.primary_exchange,
    a.underly_sec_cusip,
    a.frst_call_strk_pr,
    upper(a.primary_symbol) symbol,
    fb_proc.get_date(b.record_dt) record_dt,
    'USD' ntv_country_cd,
    b.s_p_rating,
    b.moody_rating
FROM   (SELECT a_in.*,
        rank() over(PARTITION BY a_in.cusip ORDER BY
a_in.record_seq_num DESC) rnk
    FROM   fb_prs_desc_a a_in) a
LEFT    JOIN fb_prs_desc_b b ON b.record_seq_num =
a.record_seq_num
        AND   b.cusip = a.cusip
LEFT   JOIN (SELECT --/*+ FULL(fim_in) FULL(fo)*/
        fim_in.*,
```

fo.expiration_dt,
fo.instr_master_id fo_instr_master_id
FROM   fi_instr_master fim_in
LEFT   JOIN fi_option fo ON fim_in.instr_master_id
= fo.instr_master_id
WHERE rownum > 0
AND   fim_in.data_prov_id IN (11, 23)
AND   fim_in.definer_id IS NULL) fim ON fim.cusip
= a.cusip

AND (fim.fo_instr_master_id
IS NULL

OR fim.instr_type_cd =
'RIGHTS'

OR fim.is_actv = 1)

SELECT STATEMENT, GOAL = CHOOSE
 NESTED LOOPS OUTER
  HASH JOIN OUTER
   VIEW Object owner=SMACKEY2
    TABLE ACCESS FULL Object owner=SMACKEY2 Object
name=FB_PRS_DESC_A
    TABLE ACCESS FULL Object owner=SMACKEY2 Object
name=FB_PRS_DESC_B
   VIEW Object owner=SYS
    VIEW Object owner=SMACKEY2
     COUNT
      FILTER
       NESTED LOOPS OUTER
        TABLE ACCESS BY INDEX ROWID Object
owner=SMACKEY2 Object name=FI_INSTR_MASTER
         INDEX SKIP SCAN Object owner=SMACKEY2 Object
name=FI_INSTR_MASTER_IX20
        INDEX UNIQUE SCAN Object owner=SMACKEY2 Object
name=FI_OPTION_PK

✍ ANSWER

If you mean a hash join instead of nested loops, then typically, that is determined by having enough "PGA RAM / TEMP" space to handle the hash efficiently.

"hash_area_size" or "pga_agg_target".

The optimizer parameters also play a big role. Mode of all rows is more likely to do hash than first rows. Various optimizer parameters can affect 'FTS' and index access costs to influence the CBO in one way or another.

☞ QUESTION 32

Indexes Difference

I have 2 databases, TEST and QA. The lists of tables are the same in both databases. I want to compare the indexes in these 2 databases and send the output to excel file.

Example: index1 is present in database TEST and not in QA.

Can you give me a good approach or a script?

✍ ANSWER

Within oracle, the only way to talk between two databases is to use DBlink. Unless you want to check manually, take a printout, and read line by line, strikeout whatever is matching.

Then, spool the output and do a diff in OS level (or whatever tool you have in your OS) like this:

        oracle@mutation#cat file1
        IndexName
        oracle@mutation#cat file2
        index_name
        oracle@mutation#diff file1 file2
        1c1
        < IndexName
        ---
        index_name

It also depends on your database naming conventions. Assuming two schema's, SCOTT and TEST as different databases, and you want to compare their indexes.

Here, both schemas have the same table and index on the same column, but the index name will be different.

> scott@9i > create table foo (id number primary key);
>
> Table created.
>
> scott@9i > select index_name from user_indexes;
>
> INDEX_NAME
> ---------------------------
> SYS_C001575
>
> scott@9i > !sqlplus -s test/test
> Enter value for gname: test
> test > create table foo (id number primary key);
>
> Table created.
>
> test > select index_name from user_indexes;
>
> INDEX_NAME
> ---------------------------
> SYS_C001577

If you had created the indexes as in this case, then the above SQL will generate the correct list.

> scott@9i > create table foo (id number);
>
> Table created.

scott@9i > alter table foo add constraint pk_1 primary key (id);

Table altered.

scott@9i > select index_name from user_indexes;
INDEX_NAME

PK_1

Another solution is to compare two databases' physical model, with high level tools such as ErWin. If it's not easy for you, then you can try an algorithm as follows:

First, database and etalon schema:

```
create table my_indexes
as
select *
 from user_indexes;
```

Then export table "my_indexes" from etalon schema.

Second, database and compared schema. Import given table "my_indexes" into compared schema. Then use the queries like:

Prompt compare current schema with etalon.

```
select table_name, index_name
from user_indexes
minus
select table_name, index_name
 from my_indexes;
```

Prompt and vice versa as you want.

```
select table_name, index_name
  from user_indexes
minus
select table_name, index_name
 from my_indexes;
```

☞ QUESTION 33

Prove plan invalidations

I know that gathering statistics invalidates parsed query plans for associated objects. How can I prove this?

I tried looking at invalidation counts in 'v$sql', and I didn't had any luck. I haven't checked the 9i docs yet, but the 10g didn't help either. Am I looking in the wrong place? Can you give me the right direction, or have a test case?

✍ ANSWER

Update. It appears the problem was the "no_invalidations" parameter to the "dbms_stats" package, which changes default values when moving from 9i to 10g. 10g actually appears to behave better, and as a result it wasn't invalidating the plan when the statistics were gathered, which in this case was the right thing to do. So here is the proof:

MYDBA@ORCL >
MYDBA@ORCL > – watch out for the no_invalidations param to dbms_stats which changes default value
MYDBA@ORCL > -- when moving from 9i to 10g! Used analyze table command to bypass this issue,
MYDBA@ORCL > – although could have adjusted the value of this param instead.
MYDBA@ORCL >
MYDBA@ORCL > col sql_text format a50
MYDBA@ORCL >
MYDBA@ORCL > alter system flush shared_pool;

System altered.

MYDBA@ORCL >
MYDBA@ORCL > create table crazy_table(a, b) as select rownum, 'x' from all_objects where rownum <= 1000;

Table created.

MYDBA@ORCL > create index idx on crazy_table(a);

Index created.

MYDBA@ORCL >
MYDBA@ORCL > --exec dbms_stats.gather_table_ stats(user,'crazy_table',cascade=>true,method_opt=>'for all columns size 250');
MYDBA@ORCL > analyze table crazy_table compute statistics;

Table analyzed.

MYDBA@ORCL >
MYDBA@ORCL > select * from crazy_table where a = 10;

```
    A B
--------- -
   10 x
```

1 row selected.

MYDBA@ORCL >
MYDBA@ORCL > select sql_text, invalidations from v$sql where sql_text like 'select * from crazy_table%';

SQL_TEXT   INVALIDATIONS

```
----------------------------------------- -----------
select * from crazy_table where a = 10            0
```
1 row selected.

MYDBA@ORCL >
MYDBA@ORCL > select * from crazy_table where a = 10;

```
    A B
------- -
   10 x
```

1 row selected.

MYDBA@ORCL >
MYDBA@ORCL > select sql_text, invalidations from v$sql
where sql_text like 'select * from crazy_table%';

```
SQL_TEXT                              INVALIDATIONS
----------------------------------------- -----------
select * from crazy_table where a = 10            0
```

1 row selected.

MYDBA@ORCL >
MYDBA@ORCL > --exec   dbms_stats.gather_table_
stats(user,'crazy_table',cascade=>true,method_opt=>'for
all columns size 250');
MYDBA@ORCL > analyze table crazy_table compute
statistics;

Table analyzed.

MYDBA@ORCL >
MYDBA@ORCL > select sql_text, invalidations from v$sql
where sql_text like 'select * from crazy_table%';

SQL_TEXT   INVALIDATIONS
--- ------------
select * from crazy_table where a = 10   1

1 row selected.

MYDBA@ORCL >
MYDBA@ORCL > drop table crazy_table;

Table dropped.

MYDBA@ORCL >
MYDBA@ORCL > set echo off;

☞ **QUESTION 34**

To see the optimized SQL by CBO

If I write a very complex SQL statement, I know that CBO makes it optimized by rewriting the query internally.

How do I actually see this 'optimized' query?

✍ **ANSWER**

Oracle doesn't change the physical query syntax, it just picks the optimal execution plan (or the plan it thinks is optimal). You can look at the plan by running an explain plan. You can also check the SQL Reference Guide for details.

One exception is, when you create Materialized Views and enable oracle's query rewrite feature. In such case, you need to enable SQL tracing to see the rewritten statements.

☞ QUESTION 35

AUM in Oracle

We have some sessions which use large amounts of undo, but we are not sure how large it is.

How can I determine the size of a record/s that can be updated. Is it through insert or delete?

✍ ANSWER

When user commits or rollbacks the transaction, undo segment frees the memory which was held by the old image of the record. In automatic undo management, oracle decides by itself by doing load balancing that use the undo segment.

The size of the record is equal to the size of the column which forms the record.

☞ **QUESTION 36**

Use of PCTfree, Initran, and Maxtran to prevent contention

I'm trying to decrease high I/O due to contention and concurrence of my app creates. I tested with 4K block size and the results were much better. I ended up with a lot of unused memory over a period of time, as the ASM doesn't apply to the "4K_buffers". Usually, this memory will be moved automatically to the other areas in SGA where it was needed. Now, it was hardly allocated.

I decided to stick with a 8K block and tried to use "PCTFree/ initran/maxtran".

Each process flow can do 20-30 inserts, and about 30-40 selects, with only 1 or 2 updates. It then repeats the same. Three of the longest time consuming statements in 'StatPack' are inserts. There's no trigger, FK, or too many indexes on this tables. There are about 70 to 90 processes doing this at the same time, and selecting from the same tables at the same time. In Oracle 9i, I had great success with setting up high freelist/groups, but this is not possible with auto undo management in 10g.

I need some help in the right sizing.
My set up is:
PCTFree = 60
initran = 96
maxtran = 500

These are the number of processes I'm running, are these reasonable numbers?

I know it means a lot of disk space, but this is cheap today. I have plenty of server memory - 32GB - 20 for "SGA_target".

I can see that oracle 10g ignores the maxtrans. I read somewhere on the web that this is possible, but I do not remember reading this in Oracle's 10g manuals.

What will be the down sides of this set up? Is there something I need to monitor carefully?

✍ ANSWER

You can look more at your actual transactions. You do lots of individual inserts and selects. Maybe you can combine these into fewer overall statements and do 10 larger selects instead of 10 smaller ones.

You may be too worried about instance tuning, but not worried enough about application tuning. The 'pctfree' is really just reserving space in each block so that a subsequent update will have room, in case the update causes the row size to increase oracle won't have to cause the row to "overflow" somewhere else. It makes the update result of the row to stay in the same spot. If you don't do many updates, and don't involve increase in data type sizes, like a varchar2(90) going from a content of 5 bytes to a content of 90 bytes, then you don't have to worry.

Also, I wouldn't relate freelists with undo space that would correspond more to rollback space. You may have a situation where it would be better to stick with manual segment space management, but that should not be your primary focus of activity.

I find it best to put constraints when appropriate. They may not be null, foreign key, or primary key. They provide more information to the CBO and allow the possibility of making optimizations.

In earlier releases, the maxtrans parameter determined the maximum number of concurrent update transactions allowed for each data block in the segment. This parameter was deprecated. Oracle now automatically allows up to 255 concurrent update transactions for any data block, depending on the available space in the block.

Existing objects for the value of maxtrans was already set to retain that setting. However, if you attempt to change the value for maxtrans, oracle ignores the new specification and substitutes the value 255 without returning an error.

☞ QUESTION **37**

Procedure tuning

How can I tune a procedure containing a lot of SQL in it? This procedure took 10 hours to complete the execution, but the data it's working, on are millions of records.

Can you give me a brief idea about Procedure Tuning?

✍ **ANSWER**

Tuning 'plsql' that contains a lot of SQL statements boils down to just tuning the individual SQL statements.

Try to do as much as possible in your SQL statements, rather than using multiple cursors and looping through them one row at a time, going back and forth (context switching) between plsql and SQL.

Just do one large SQL statement one at a time. If you do need to process the data a row at a time in plsql, then use the bulk collect feature to operate on chunks of rows. Bulk them into a collection, then loop through that array, process, then bulk collect some more.

Try to check if there are small SQL statements that can be combined into a single statement. From statement, it could be turned into an insert, and then into select. You can do it through accomplishing it in a single SQL statement. If it's not possible, do it in multiple SQL statements. As a last resort, use plsql cursors and looping constructs, but do those in bulk as much as possible.

☞ **QUESTION 38**

bigger block size for indexes help increase performance and lower I/O

I have a high I/O activity due to a 3rd party application which is not under my control. I used in the past 32KA block size for indexes to improve the performance to have good results. The application support said that they are too competent in Oracle, but not to expect better results because of the "application's nature".

Here is what the app does:

It reads from a file 1 record at the time, inserts different parts of this record into 6-7 major tables. It selects from the same tables to compare the sets If there are matches, it inserts into audit tables. Every new record creates a search for matches as well. There are also 3-4 history tables for each record processed. It's not a big deal, but there are up to 70 processes running this app simultaneously. The I/O and concurrency come from inserting and selecting from the same tables and the number of sessions. I cannot change this because it's produced by a third party.

My question is, am I going to get better performance if I move the indexes to the 32K block size? Ora 10.1.0.4, aix5.2, 12Gb server ram, and a block size for all - 8K. Right now, it's running with 6GB for SGA and about 3GB for PGA. There are also multiple processes running and selecting randomly small amount of data to compare. If I decrease the size for the table data to 2K, is this going to affect my performance as well?

✍ ANSWER

You should run a test with 32k and 2k block size, and then compare the difference . Maybe a third at 8k, run a copy of the app in QA, and benchmark it. That takes all the "in theory" stuff and puts it to the test. With that, it's better to have smaller block size.

The advantage is it is going to cause less contention for simultaneous small modification processes, at both the disk and latch/enqueue level. This is due to less information stored on each block.

It would cause less I/O on small single row select statements, because if you need only one row of data, you would only be reading 2K of info. It would use most of it rather than reading 32K then ignoring most of it.

In addition to that, if you have small single row queries that are using index access, and the queries are running often enough, then once the index block is brought into the buffer cache, it can be used to service many queries since it has many index entries in it. It will be less I/O to disk.

Buffer busy waits may be a problem for a high transactional index but a larger intrans and maxtrans can mitigate that.

☞ QUESTION 39

Tuning SQL by using explain plan

How can I tune and rewrite this statement?

explain plan for
SELECT /*+ first_rows */
i.ACTUAL_PURCHASE_PRICE,
i.COMM_ID,
cd.CONTRACT_OID LAST_CONTRACT_OID,
c.CONTRACT_ID LAST_CONTRACT_ID,
cd.EFFECTIVE_DATE,
cd.START_DATE,
i.LIST_PRICE,
i.LOCATION_OID,
i.ORDER_NUMBER,
i.QTY,
i.SERIAL_NUMBER,
i.SERIAL_NUMBER_LK,
i.SHIP_DATE,
i.SO_LINE_NUM,
i.OID,
i.VERSION,
i.PO_NUMBER,
p.PRODUCT_ID,
p.PRODUCT_ID_LK,
p.PRODUCT_NAME,
P.PRODUCT_NUMBER,
P.STATUS PRODUCT_STATUS,
cd.COVERAGE_TYPE_OID,
cd.SERV_PART_NUMBER,
c.BUYER_COMPANY_OID,
ct.COVERAGE_NAME ,

L.SELLER_COM_OID,
L.COMPANY_ID,
L.COMPANY_STATUS,
L.STATE_NAME,
L.STATE_CODE,
(
select quote_id
from SAM_quote q
where q.creation_date =
(
select max(q.creation_date)
from SAM_quote q , SAM_quote_detail qd
where q.OID = qd.quote_oid
and i.oid = qd.INS_PRODUCT_OID
)
and rownum < 2
) latest_quote_id ,
(
select oid from SAM_quote q
where q.creation_date =
(
select max(q.creation_date)
from SAM_quote q , SAM_quote_detail qd
where q.OID = qd.quote_oid
and i.oid = qd.INS_PRODUCT_OID
)
and rownum < 2
) latest_quote_oid ,
(
select opportunity_id from SAM_opportunity o
where o.created_time =
(
select max(o.created_time)
from SAM_opportunity o , SAM_opportunity_detail Od
where O.OID = Od.opportunity_oid

```
and i.oid = Od.INSTALLED_PRODUCT_OID
)
and rownum < 2
) latest_opportunity_id ,
(
select oid from SAM_opportunity o
where o.created_time =
(
select max(o.created_time)
from SAM_opportunity o , SAM_opportunity_detail Od
where O.OID = Od.opportunity_oid
and i.oid = Od.INSTALLED_PRODUCT_OID
)
and rownum < 2
) latest_opportunity_oid
FROM INV_PRODUCT i,
CON_DETAIL cd,
CON c,
PRODUCT p,
LOC l,
COV_TYPE ct
WHERE i.last_contract_detail_oid = cd.oid(+) AND
NVL(cd.contract_oid,-99999) = c.oid(+) AND
L.oid = i.location_oid AND
p.oid = i.product_oid AND
cd.COVERAGE_TYPE_OID = ct.oid(+)
and i.serial_number_lk like '%'

    1 select operation, options, object_name
    2 from plan_table
    3* connect by prior id=parent_id and prior statement_id
      = statement_id
SQL>
SQL> /
```

OPERATION OPTIONS OBJECT_NAME
---------------------------- -------------------------- --------------------------
SELECT STATEMENT
COUNT STOPKEY
NESTED LOOPS OUTER
NESTED LOOPS
NESTED LOOPS OUTER
NESTED LOOPS OUTER
NESTED LOOPS
NESTED LOOPS
NESTED LOOPS
NESTED LOOPS OUTER
NESTED LOOPS
TABLE ACCESS FULL SAM_COUNTRY
TABLE ACCESS BY INDEX ROWID SAM_LOCATION
INDEX RANGE SCAN IDX_LOCATION_10
TABLE ACCESS BY INDEX ROWID SAM_STATE
INDEX UNIQUE SCAN PK_STATE
TABLE ACCESS BY INDEX ROWID COMPANY
INDEX UNIQUE SCAN PK_COMPANY
TABLE ACCESS BY INDEX ROWID INV_PRODUCT
INDEX RANGE SCAN IDX_INSTALLED_PRODUCT_06
TABLE ACCESS BY INDEX ROWID SAM_PRODUCT
INDEX UNIQUE SCAN PK_PRODUCT
TABLE ACCESS BY INDEX ROWID CON_DETAIL
INDEX UNIQUE SCAN PK_CONTRACT_DETAIL
TABLE ACCESS BY INDEX ROWID COV_TYPE
INDEX UNIQUE SCAN PK_COVERAGE_TYPE
TABLE ACCESS BY INDEX ROWID SAM_COMPANY
INDEX UNIQUE SCAN PK_COMPANY
TABLE ACCESS BY INDEX ROWID CON
INDEX UNIQUE SCAN PK_CONTRACT

✍ ANSWER

You can try the following, but it's an untested code.

```
SELECT /*+ FIRST_ROWS */
      i.actual_purchase_price
,     i.comm_id
,     cd.contract_oid        last_contract_oid
,     c.contract_id          last_contract_id
,     cd.effective_date
,     cd.start_date
,     i.list_price
,     i.location_oid
,     i.order_number
,     i.qty
,     i.serial_number
,     i.serial_number_lk
,     i.ship_date
,     i.so_line_num
,     i.oid
,     i.version
,     i.po_number
,     p.product_id
,     p.product_id_lk
,     p.product_name
,     p.product_number
,     p.status product_status
,     cd.coverage_type_oid
,     cd.serv_part_number
,     c.buyer_company_oid
,     ct.coverage_name
,     l.seller_com_oid
,     l.company_id
,     l.company_status
,     l.state_name
```

```
,      l.state_code
,      qmax.quote_id          latest_quote_id
,      qmax.oid               latest_quote_oid
,      ip.opportunity_id      latest_opportunity_id
,      ip.oid                 latest_opportunity_oid
FROM   inv_product        i
,      con_detail         cd
,      con                c
,      product            p
,      loc                l
,      cov_type           ct
,      (SELECT  a.ins_product_oid
        ,     a.quote_id
        ,     a.oid
        FROM   (SELECT qd.ins_product_oid
              ,      q.quote_id
              ,      q.oid
              ,      q.creation_date
              ,      MAX(q.creation_date)
                      OVER (PARTITION BY qd.ins_product_oid)
max_creation_date
              ,      ROW_NUMBER()
                      OVER (PARTITION BY qd.ins_product_oid
                          ORDER BY    q.creation_date DESC) rnk
              FROM    sam_quote       q
              ,      sam_quote_detail  qd
              WHERE   q.oid = q.quote_oid) a
        WHERE   a.creation_date = a.max_creation_date
        AND     a.rnk        = 1) qmax
,      (SELECT  b.installed_product_id
        ,     b.opportunity_id
        ,     b.oid
        FROM   (SELECT od.installed_product_id
              ,      o.opportunity_id
              ,      o.oid
```

```
              ,     o.created_time
              ,     MAX(o.created_time)
                 OVER (PARTITION BY od.installed_product_id)
max_created_time
              ,     ROW_NUMBER()
                 OVER (PARTITION BY od.installed_product_id
                    ORDER BY    o.created_time DESC) rnk
          FROM    sam_opportunity       o
              ,     sam_opportunity_detail  od
          WHERE   od.opportunity_oid = o.oid) b
      WHERE   b.created_time = b.max_created_time
      AND    b.rnk        = 1) ip
WHERE   i.last_contract_detail_oid  = cd.oid (+)
AND    NVL(cd.contract_oid,-99999) = c.oid (+)
AND    l.oid             = i.location_oid
AND    p.oid             = i.product_oid
AND    cd.coverage_type_oid      = ct.oid (+)
AND    i.serial_number_lk       IS NOT NULL
AND    i.oid             = ip.installed_product_oid (+)
AND    i.oid             = qmax.ins_product_oid (+)
```

☞ QUESTION 40

"slave shutdown wait" – event

I'm looking for information on this wait event: "slave shutdown wait".

Where can I find information on this?

✍ ANSWER

It can be found in 10gR1 docs. "PX server shutdown".

During normal or immediate shutdown, the parallel execution slaves are posted to shutdown cleanly. If any parallel execution slaves are still running after 10 seconds, they are executed. Waiting period for that is up to 0.5 seconds.

Parameter Description
Nalive = The number of parallel execution slaves that are still running.
Sleeptime = The total sleep time from the start of the session's wait for this event.
Loop = The number of times the session waited for this event.
During shutdown, immediate or normal, the shutdown process must wait for all the dispatchers to shutdown. As each dispatcher is signaled, the session that causes the shutdown waits on this event until the requested dispatcher is no longer running. Waiting period for this is 1 second

"Waited" indicates the cumulative wait time. After 5 minutes, the session writes to the alert and trace files to indicate that there might be a problem.

☞ QUESTION 41

Oracle 9i function base index

Our java application is storing data in some of the columns in mixed cases. For some reasons that I am not aware of, we have function-based indexes on some of these columns. In Oracle9i documentation, I read that Function-based indexes is defined with the "UPPER(column_name)" or "LOWER(column_name)" keywords which allow case-insensitive searches. I looked into our code and noticed none of the SELECT query statements are against these columns which use "UPPER()" or "LOWER()" functions in the WHERE clause. SQL trace file shows that Oracle9i is not using these indexes.

Do we really need function-based indexes on columns with mixed case data? Should we drop these function-based indexes and create normal indexes instead, since our code is not using "UPPER(column_name)" or "LOWER(column_ name)" functions in the where clauses? Does using functions in our select query statements and having function-based indexes, have an effect on the performance?

✍ ANSWER

If you have a regular index, it will store the actual key values in the column that sounds like mixed case. If a query does a comparison using the exact same mixed case, then the index would be used (in theory, cbo determines if appropriate). If your where clause used "upper(col) = upper(val)", then the index could not be used. If you indexed "upper(col)", as in a function based index, then it could.

Perhaps the best way to explain is like this:
MYDBA@ORCL >
MYDBA@ORCL > create table test(a varchar2(30));

Table created.

MYDBA@ORCL >
MYDBA@ORCL > insert into test values ('HEllo');

1 row created.

MYDBA@ORCL > commit;

Commit complete.

MYDBA@ORCL >
MYDBA@ORCL > create index reg_idx on test(a);
Index created.

MYDBA@ORCL > create index fbi_idx on test(upper(a));

Index created.

MYDBA@ORCL >
MYDBA@ORCL > exec dbms_stats.gather_table_stats(us
er,'test',cascade=>true,method_opt=>'for all columns size
250');

PL/SQL procedure successfully completed.

MYDBA@ORCL >
MYDBA@ORCL > set autotrace on explain;
MYDBA@ORCL >

MYDBA@ORCL > select * from test where a = 'hello';

no rows selected
Execution Plan

---

    0   SELECT STATEMENT Optimizer=ALL_ROWS (Cost=1
Card=1 Bytes=6)
    1   0   INDEX (RANGE SCAN) OF 'REG_IDX' (INDEX)
(Cost=1 Card=1 Bytes=6)

MYDBA@ORCL >
MYDBA@ORCL > select * from test where a = 'HELLO';

no rows selected

Execution Plan

---

    0   SELECT STATEMENT Optimizer=ALL_ROWS (Cost=1
Card=1 Bytes=6)
    1   0   INDEX (RANGE SCAN) OF 'REG_IDX' (INDEX)
(Cost=1 Card=1 Bytes=6)

MYDBA@ORCL >
MYDBA@ORCL > select * from test where a = 'HEllo';
A

HEllo

1 row selected.

Execution Plan

---

    0   SELECT STATEMENT Optimizer=ALL_ROWS (Cost=1
Card=1 Bytes=6)
    1   0   INDEX (RANGE SCAN) OF 'REG_IDX' (INDEX)

(Cost=1 Card=1 Bytes=6)

MYDBA@ORCL >
MYDBA@ORCL > select * from test where upper(a) = 'HEllo';

no rows selected

Execution Plan
----
  0   SELECT STATEMENT Optimizer=ALL_ROWS (Cost=2 Card=1 Bytes=6)
  1   0   TABLE ACCESS (BY INDEX ROWID) OF 'TEST' (TABLE) (Cost=2 Card=1 Bytes=6)
  2   1   INDEX (RANGE SCAN) OF 'FBI_IDX' (INDEX) (Cost=1 Card=1)

MYDBA@ORCL >
MYDBA@ORCL > select * from test where upper(a) = 'HELLO';

A

HEllo

1 row selected.

Execution Plan
----
  0   SELECT STATEMENT Optimizer=ALL_ROWS (Cost=2 Card=1 Bytes=6)
  1   0   TABLE ACCESS (BY INDEX ROWID) OF 'TEST' (TABLE) (Cost=2 Card=1 Bytes=6)
  2   1   INDEX (RANGE SCAN) OF 'FBI_IDX' (INDEX) (Cost=1 Card=1)

MYDBA@ORCL >
MYDBA@ORCL > set autotrace off;
MYDBA@ORCL > drop table test;

Table dropped.

MYDBA@ORCL > set echo off;

☞ QUESTION 42

Query tuning with NVL

How can I rewrite this query, especially the NVL part, as I can't index it?
SELECT   *
FROM   hsd_accounts_payable
WHERE   file_type = NVL (:b6, file_type)
AND
(
(select_for_payment = 'S' AND ap_status IN ('F', 'R')
)
OR
(select_for_payment = 'U' AND ap_status = 'H')
)
AND
ap_type = :b5 AND
company_code = :b4
AND NVL(schedule_id, ROWID) =
DECODE(:b3,NULL, NVL(schedule_id, ROWID),:b3)
AND
NVL(vendor_group_id, ROWID) = DECODE(:b2,
                              NULL, NVL(vendor_group_id,
ROWID),
                              :b2)
AND   SubStr(NVL(payment_method,'B'),1,1)   =   Decode(:
b1,'Y','R','B')
ORDER BY   seq_vend_id, seq_vend_address,file_type, seq_
claim_id
FOR UPDATE

plan is like

Id	Operation	Name	Rows	Bytes	Cost
0	SELECT STATEMENT			2	414	133K
1	FOR UPDATE					
2	SORT ORDER BY		2	414	133K
3	CONCATENATION					
4	FILTER					
5	TABLE ACCESS BY INDEX ROWID	ACCOUNTS_PAYABLE	1	207	66965	
6	INDEX RANGE SCAN	ACC_PAY#CC#APTY#SFP#APST	1485K	5812	
7	FILTER					
8	TABLE ACCESS BY INDEX ROWID	ACCOUNTS_PAYABLE	1	207	66965	
9	INDEX RANGE SCAN	ACC_PAY#CC#APTY#SFP#APST	1485K	5812	

✍ ANSWER

You can always use function based indexes.

Example:

SQL> CREATE TABLE x (c1 NUMBER);

Table created.

SQL>
SQL> INSERT INTO x VALUES (NULL);
1 row created.

SQL>

SQL> INSERT INTO x VALUES (1);

1 row created.

SQL>
SQL> CREATE INDEX x_idx ON x(nvl(c1, 999));

Index created.

SQL>
SQL> EXPLAIN PLAN FOR SELECT /*+INDEX(x)*/ * FROM
x where nvl(c1, 999) = 999;

Explained.

SQL>
SQL> SELECT * FROM table(DBMS_XPLAN.DISPLAY);

PLAN_TABLE_OUTPUT

| Id | Operation | Name | Rows | Bytes | Cost (%CPU)|

| 0 | SELECT STATEMENT | | 1 | 13 | 2 (50)|
| 1 | TABLE ACCESS BY INDEX ROWID| X | | 1 | 13
| 2 (50)|
|* 2 | INDEX RANGE SCAN | X_IDX | 1 | | 1 (0)|

Predicate Information (identified by operation id):

PLAN_TABLE_OUTPUT
----

2 - access(NVL("X"."C1",999)=999)

13 rows selected.

☞ QUESTION 43

Checkpoint is running slow

Is there a way to figure out if dBWR is taking too long to flush dirty buffers to the datafiles? I read that check pointing occurs every 3 seconds or earlier, if there is a switch in log file. How can I figure out when the checkpoint occurs in reference to data files? I believe datafile header only keeps the most current checkpoint number. If the buffer cache size (db_cache_size in 9i) is too high, is there a chance that check pointing will be running slow, even for the same number of dml transactions as compared to a smaller size buffer cache?

✍ ANSWER

The "LOG_CHECKPOINTS_TO_ALERT" 'init.ora' parameter, when set to a value of TRUE, allows you to log checkpoint start and stop times in the alert log. This is very helpful in determining if checkpoints are occurring at the optimal frequency, and gives a chronological view of checkpoints, and other database activities occurring in the background.

☞ **QUESTION 44**

Users and default optimizer_mode

On a system that I've taken over, the developers have one user account that has "optimizer_mode" as rule when they log-on. They have another that has choose. I thought that the optimizer mode could only be set within the 'init.ora' hint or alter system command.

Is there a role that can set this as default for a user when they log-on?

✍ **ANSWER**

There's an AFTER LOGON trigger, setting it using "ALTER SESSION".

i.e. "SQL> ALTER SESSION SET OPTIMIZER_MODE = FIRST_ROWS;"

   Session altered.

You need to identify the trigger, and figure out why it's doing that.

☞ QUESTION 45

Rewrite a query

I have a query, very simple, but it is time consuming. There
are indexes on each of the join fields. All indexes are analyzed
in the last 2 hours with "GATHER_TABLE_STATS".
 Here is the query and the execution plan:
SELECT inv_id
FROM p_inventory pi, p_project_unit ppu
WHERE pi.unit_num = ppu.unit_num
AND pi.project_id = ppu.project_id
AND pi.project_id = 240
AND pi.season_code = :b1
AND ppu.unit_type_code = :b2
AND oeb_code = :b3
AND inv_status_code = 0
AND NOT EXISTS (
SELECT /*+ INDEX(P_CONTRACT_PURCHASE CONTRPR_
INV_FK_I)*/ 1
FROM p_contract_purchase pcp, p_contract pc
WHERE pcp.inv_id = pi.inv_id
AND pc.contr_num = pcp.contr_num
AND pc.current_contr_status NOT IN ('ICL', 'CXL'))
AND ROWNUM <= 1
ORDER BY inv_id ASC;

Operation Object Name Rows Bytes Cost Object Node In/
Out PStart PStop

SELECT STATEMENT Optimizer Mode=CHOOSE 1 636
SORT ORDER BY 1 5 K 636
COUNT STOPKEY
HASH JOIN ANTI 161 5 K 633 :Q174489006 P->S QC

(RANDOM)
HASH JOIN 161 5 K 28 :Q174489004 P->P HASH
TABLE ACCESS FULL PREMIER.P_PROJECT_UNIT 436 5
K 4 :Q174489000 S->P HASH
TABLE ACCESS FULL PREMIER.P_INVENTORY 953 20 K
23 :Q174489002 P->P HASH
VIEW SYS.VW_SQ_1 524 K 1 M 604 :Q174489005 P->P
HASH
HASH JOIN 524 K 7 M 604 :Q174489005 PCWP
INDEX FAST FULL SCAN PREMIER.P_CONTRACT_
CURRENT_STATUS_I 483 K 3 M 249 :Q174489001 S->P
HASH
TABLE ACCESS FULL PREMIER.P_CONTRACT_
PURCHASE 878 K 5 M 216 :Q174489003 P->P HASH
CREATE TABLE P_INVENTORY (
INV_ID NUMBER(12) NOT NULL,
PROJECT_ID VARCHAR2(4 BYTE) NOT NULL,
UNIT_NUM VARCHAR2(6 BYTE) NOT NULL,
SEASON_CODE VARCHAR2(3 BYTE) NOT NULL,
INV_STATUS_CODE VARCHAR2(3 BYTE) NOT NULL,
ELEMENT VARCHAR2(3 BYTE) NOT NULL,
OEB_CODE VARCHAR2(1 BYTE) NOT NULL);
CREATE TABLE P_CONTRACT_PURCHASE (
CONTR_NUM NUMBER(12) NOT NULL,
PURCHASE_ID NUMBER(3) NOT NULL,
PROJECT_ID VARCHAR2(4 BYTE),
INV_ID NUMBER(12));
CREATE INDEX CONTRPR_INV_FK_I ON P_CONTRACT_
PURCHASE
(INV_ID);

CREATE TABLE P_PROJECT_UNIT (
PROJECT_ID VARCHAR2(4 BYTE) NOT NULL,
UNIT_NUM VARCHAR2(6 BYTE) NOT NULL);

CREATE UNIQUE INDEX PRJUNT_PK ON P_PROJECT_
UNIT
(PROJECT_ID, UNIT_NUM);
CREATE UNIQUE INDEX INV_PK ON P_INVENTORY
(INV_ID);
CREATE UNIQUE INDEX INV_UK ON P_INVENTORY
(PROJECT_ID, UNIT_NUM, ELEMENT, OEB_CODE);

✍ Answer

Using an index is not necessarily the fastest execution method.
If the table is small, then a full table scan is usually faster. That
is why the optimizer chooses to do a full table scan, instead of
using an index. When comparing queries, the best measure is
timed tests, not whether it is using an index or what the cost
is. Since you do not care which row is returned, then you do
not need the min.

You can test the following.

```
SELECT pi.inv_id
FROM   p_inventory pi, p_project_unit ppu,
    (SELECT pcp.inv_id
    FROM   p_contract_purchase pcp, p_contract pc
    WHERE  pc.contr_num = pcp.contr_num
    AND    pc.current_contr_status NOT IN ('ICL', 'CXL')) p
WHERE  pi.unit_num = ppu.unit_num
AND    pi.project_id = ppu.project_id
AND    pi.project_id = 240
AND    pi.season_code = :b1
AND    ppu.unit_type_code = :b2
AND    oeb_code = :b3
AND    inv_status_code = 0
AND    pi.inv_id = p.inv_id (+)
```

AND   p.inv_id IS NULL
AND   ROWNUM <= 1
/

You can also try to add "rownum > 0" to the inline view to materialize it.

```
SELECT pi.inv_id
FROM   p_inventory pi, p_project_unit ppu,
    (SELECT pcp.inv_id
     FROM   p_contract_purchase pcp, p_contract pc
     WHERE  pc.contr_num = pcp.contr_num
     AND    pc.current_contr_status NOT IN ('ICL', 'CXL')
     AND    ROWNUM > 0) p
WHERE  pi.unit_num = ppu.unit_num
AND    pi.project_id = ppu.project_id
AND    pi.project_id = 240
AND    pi.season_code = :b1
AND    ppu.unit_type_code = :b2
AND    oeb_code = :b3
AND    inv_status_code = 0
AND    pi.inv_id = p.inv_id (+)
AND    p.inv_id IS NULL
AND    ROWNUM <= 1
/
```

☞ QUESTION 46

Production database to test environment for load tests

We have to test and produce the same hardware and disk sizes.

Now, we want to move the production data to the test environment. An export and import will "destroy" the fragmentation of the Oracle data files.

How can we copy the data files? What disadvantages do we have to consider?

✎ ANSWER

With DMT, you can use "pctincrease=0" and "initial=next". With LMT, you can use uniform extent size because there is absolutely no fragmentation.

To copy the data files, you can use RMAN to duplicate the PROD to TEST. The disadvantage is you could copy the cloning.

Have a backup of control file, (backup control file to trace) shutdown your production, copy all the files to a new location, and rebuild the control files.

☞ QUESTION 47

Foreign key vs. Custom Scripts

My database vendor insists on using scripts in order to keep
consistence in table relations. The foreign keys were made
to do this job, but it is not affecting the performance.

Where can I find documentation?

✍ ANSWER

Relational databases are made for this (tables level
constraints).

Handling constraints/foreign-key in application (procedures/
triggers) is the worst recommended method. It adds too
much of work on the application.

☞ QUESTION 48

Full table scan

I have one SQL query and I also have 7 the same SQL query like this. The problem is the query is taking full table scan.

INSERT INTO load_pdr_group (
business_org
, baes_site
, emp_cat
, baes_grade
, baes_job_code
, baes_exec_marker
, employee_catg
, yesno
, baes_overtime_paid
, baes_pdr_group
, pdr_group_id
)
SELECT x.business_org
, x.baes_site
, x.emp_cat
, x.baes_grade
, x.baes_job_code
, x.baes_exec_marker
, x.employee_catg
, x.yesno
, x.baes_overtime_paid
, x.baes_pdr_group
, x.pdr_group_id
FROM (SELECT apg.business_org
, apg.baes_site
, apg.emp_cat

, apg.baes_grade
, apg.baes_job_code
, apg.baes_exec_marker
, apg.employee_catg
, apg.yesno
, apg.baes_overtime_paid
, apg.baes_pdr_group
, apg.pdr_group_id
, NVL(apg.exception,'X') exception
, NVL(apg.deleted, 'X') deleted
, MAX(apg.pdr_group_id)
OVER (PARTITION BY apg.business_org
, apg.baes_site
, apg.emp_cat
, apg.baes_grade
, apg.baes_job_code
, apg.baes_exec_marker
, apg.employee_catg
, apg.yesno
, apg.baes_overtime_paid
, apg.baes_pdr_group
, apg.pdr_group_id) max_pdr_group_id
FROM audit_pdr_group apg) x
WHERE x.pdr_group_id = x.max_pdr_group_id
AND x.exception != 'Y'
AND x.deleted != 'Y'

I have Primary key on the "pdr_group_id", and my db is
8.1.7.4.

What index should I make on this?

✍ ANSWER

A full table scan is not always bad. Sometimes, it is the fastest and most efficient path to the data. Without knowledge on distribution of data or any execution plan, statspack report, and trace analysis, we have no idea what might be actually happening (assuming the tables/indexes are analyzed and CBO is using those indexes).

☞ QUESTION 49

The best strategy to gather statistics in a dynamic way

We have a "cache" database that is used to merge data from different applications, and present them to a web front end. Most of the data is purged from the database at night. This mean, that we have many transactions during the day, and the amount of data grows during a working day.

In addition, we need DB statistics to make sure that the application performance is acceptable. We will transfer soon from Oracle 8i to Oracle 10g.

Does anyone have experience or ideas on what is the best strategy to gather db/system statistics within Oracle 10g with a system like that?

✍ ANSWER

You can look into dynamic sampling, enable table monitoring "sql> and alter table table_name monitoring". Then, your table will be analyzed only if there are a certain percentage of changes.

In your "dbms_stats" use "GATHER STALE" then, look into "GATHER_SYTEM_STATS".

You should also note that monitoring option is depreciated in 10g. The right approach is enabling automatic statistics gathering.

☞ QUESTION 50

Use of more disk space in executing query

I can find the SQL text (i.e. query) which uses more disk space, but I want to know which user is executing that query.

The query is as follows:

SQL>Select sql_TEXT, DISK_READS FROM V$SQLAREA ORDER BY DISK_READS DESC;

Get the first 10 SQL where disk reads are highest, and get first 10 SQL where "buffer_gets" are highest.

Which one uses the most disk space?

✍ ANSWER

Select "sql_TEXT, DISK_READS FROM V$SQLAREA ORDER BY DISK_READS DESC;"

change to:

"Select   username,sql_TEXT,   DISK_READS   FROM V$SQLAREA, dba_users

where parsing_user_id = user_id ORDER BY DISK_READS DESC;"

☞ QUESTION 51

Document security model

I'm working on a project that requires implementation of document security model in application. Document may be for public or private use. We have a document table, which contains document information, document ID (numeric), and bit flag PUBLIC/PRIVATE (PPFlag).

We also have ACL table which contains pairs "documentedID" and "userID/usergroupID". Based on the functional requirements, we need to show to the users a portion of accessible documents sorted by some fields (user selects sorting field), and implement navigation PREV/NEXT Page.

ACL Table Structure:
UserID - int - contains UserID od UserGroupID
DocID - int - document ID
UserOrGroupFlag - bit - contains flag the record for user or users' group

Our select looks like the following:

SELECT * FROM (SELECT Field1, Field2 FROM DocumentTable DT
WHERE (((PPFlag = 0
OR EXISTS (SELECT 1 FROM ACL WHERE docID = DT.DocID
AND(UserID={current_user_id}ANDUSERORGROUPFLAG = 1
OR EXISTS (SELECT 1 FROM UserGroups ug WHERE ug.UserGroupID = UserID
AND EXISTS (SELECT 1 FROM User_UserGroups uug

WHERE uug.UserGroupID = ug.UserGroupID AND uug.
UserLoginID = {current_user_id}))))))))
ORDER BY UPPER(SomeField) ASC, DocID ASC) WHERE
ROWNUM<=26

This query shows a slow performance with the millions of
records in Document Table and ACL tables.

After performance investigation, we removed all OR
operations from query by using "UNION ALL". We also
removed usage of "User_UserGroups" table, because
we know that all groups in which current user consist,
implements checking. As for the user, it also used "UNION
ALL" operation. For the final step, we renormalize sorting
data to remove function "UPPER" in "ORDER BY" clause.
After all this improvements, we get a query on several
pages.

Performance of the resulting query became better, but under
the heavy load (~1000 concurrent sessions), it took a one
minute response time (we should have response time in 2-5
seconds) for millions of records in both tables.
All required indexes were added, and we also tried to use
hints, but it didn't help.

Is there a fast document security model pattern that can
improve our query/model?

✍ ANSWER

VPD may be an ideal solution. Check if the statistics are
updated and maintained properly. Certain parameters like
"pga_aggregate_target", needs to be looked into for workload
related issues.

You can also try the following:

```
select doc.doc_id, doc.doc_name, doc.doc_author, etc
from (
select doc_id from acl
where usergroup_id = myuserid and idtype = 'USER'
union
select doc_id from acl
where  usergroup_id  =  myusergroupid  and  idtype  =
'GROUP'
union
select doc_id from doc
where publicflag = 'PUBLIC'
) a, doc
where doc.id = a.doc_id
order by whatever;
```

Organize your ACL table index with user group. Your user id's and group id's should be unique. Distinguish if they need a flag to tell them apart. You can also try doing it as two tables, an associative table between documents and user id's, and another associative table between documents and user group id's. Both would be index organized with second document. Avoid making 'public' an attribute of a document, instead group all the member of the users.

☞ QUESTION **52**

Can you tell me what forced view is?

Can you tell me what forced view is?

✍ ANSWER

Force is a keyword. It forces the creation of a view even when the view will be invalid. It's a feature in 10g. It also works in 9iR2 and 10gR1.
None force is the default.
eg: assuming the table 'xyz' does not exist

CREATE FORCE VIEW view_force AS
SELECT * FROM xyz;
In addition, you can use force if you want to create the view, regardless of whether the view's base tables, the reference object types exist, or the owner of the schema containing the view has privileges on them.

These conditions must be true before any select, insert, update, or delete statements can be issued against the view.

If the view definition contains any constraints, create view force will fail if the base table does not exist, or the referenced object type does not exist. Create view force will also fail if the view definition names a constraint that does not exist.
scott@9ir2>select * from v$version;
BANNER

Oracle9i Enterprise Edition Release 9.2.0.1.0 - Production

PL/SQL Release 9.2.0.1.0 - Production
CORE 9.2.0.1.0 Production
TNS for Compaq Tru64 UNIX: Version 9.2.0.1.0 - Production
NLSRTL Version 9.2.0.1.0 - Production
scott@9ir2>desc xyz
ERROR:
ORA-04043: object xyz does not exist
scott@9ir2>CREATE FORCE VIEW view_force AS SELECT
* FROM xyz;
Warning: View created with compilation errors.
scott@9ir2>select VIEW_NAME, TEXT from user_views
where VIEW_NAME = 'VIEW_FORCE';
VIEW_NAME

TEXT

VIEW_FORCE
SELECT * FROM xyz
scott@9ir2>select * from view_force;
select * from view_force
*
ERROR at line 1:
ORA-04063: view "SCOTT.VIEW_FORCE" has errors
scott@9ir2>drop view view_force;
View dropped.
scott@9ir2>select VIEW_NAME, TEXT from user_views
where VIEW_NAME = 'VIEW_FORCE';
no rows selected

☞ QUESTION **53**

Composite bitmap indexes

Can I create a bitmap index on two columns, both with a few
distinct values?
eg:

COlumn x : values 1,2,3,4
Column y: values N,S,E,W

Does it make sense to create a composite bitmap index on
the above two columns?

✍ ANSWER

Yes, you can. It will make sense if you use conditions like
"(x=<<>> and y=<<>>) or (x=<<>> and y=<<>>)" or like
"x=<<>> or x=<<>>" (considering x is the first column in
the index).
SQL> select count(1) from bin_idx_tab;
COUNT(1)

_____

9001
SQL> select unique * from bin_idx_tab;
A B

_____ __

1 A
1 B
1 C
2 A
2 B

2 C
3 A
3 B
3 C
9 rows selected.
SQL> create bitmap index btm01 on bin_idx_tab(a,b);
Index created.
SQL> exec dbms_stats.gather_table_stats(ownname=>user,
tabname=>'bin_idx_tab', cascade=>true);
PL/SQL procedure successfully completed.
SQL> set autotrace traceonly
SQL> select * from bin_idx_tab where (a=1 and b='C') or
(a=2 and b='B');
2000 rows selected.
Execution Plan
----
0 SELECT STATEMENT Optimizer=ALL_ROWS (Cost=1
Card=2000 Bytes=
10000)
1 0 BITMAP CONVERSION (TO ROWIDS) (Cost=1 Card=2000
Bytes=1000
0)
2 1 BITMAP INDEX (FAST FULL SCAN) OF 'BTM01' (INDEX
(BITMAP)
)
Statistics
----
1 recursive calls
0 db block gets
5 consistent gets
0 physical reads
0 redo size
26852 bytes sent via SQL*Net to client
1971 bytes received via SQL*Net from client
135 SQL*Net roundtrips to/from client
0 sorts (memory)

0 sorts (disk)
2000 rows processed
SQL> drop index btm01;
Index dropped.
SQL> select * from bin_idx_tab where (a=1 and b='C') or (a=2 and b='B');
2000 rows selected.
Execution Plan

----

0 SELECT STATEMENT Optimizer=ALL_ROWS (Cost=6 Card=2000 Bytes=
10000)
1 0 TABLE ACCESS (FULL) OF 'BIN_IDX_TAB' (TABLE) (Cost=6 Card=
2000 Bytes=10000)
Statistics

----

158 recursive calls
0 db block gets
174 consistent gets
0 physical reads
0 redo size
26852 bytes sent via SQL*Net to client
1971 bytes received via SQL*Net from client
135 SQL*Net roundtrips to/from client
3 sorts (memory)
0 sorts (disk)
2000 rows processed

You also have to note that in creating a composite bitmap, you lose some flexibility with the total number of possible queries and combinations that may be useful to you. It depends of course on your situation. This is particularly true when you get to 3 or more columns. You may want to test having separate bitmaps for each column vs. one or two composite indexes.

☞ QUESTION 54

Select on some table which gives poor performance

I have procedures which select data from the same table and insert into another table. If I run them independently they run fast, but when executed simultaneously, both process execution time doubles. My expectation is that all procedures should run simultaneously without performance degradation.

I want to know if firing 'SELECT' query against same table simultaneously, through cursor, affects the performance. Is there anything I should look at, for this poor performance?

The procedure goes like this:

```
cursor cur1 is select <column_list> from
common_table,tab1,tab2,tab3
where col1=col2
and col3=col4;

type char_array is table of varchar2(200) index by binary_
integer;
num_array is table of number index by binary_integer;

begin
open cur1;
loop
begin
fetch cu1 bulk collect cur1 into
var1,var2...limit 100;
```

forall 1 in var1.first.. var1.last save exceptions
 insert into main_table(col list)
values(var1(i),var2(i),,,);

exception
when others then
insert into execption_tab(col list)
values(var list);
end;
end loop;

Only one table in cursor select query is common in all
procedures and contains around 400,000 records. Other
procedures are also of the same format except that the main
table is different.

✍ ANSWER

Use set auto trace explain only on 'sqlplus', to see the
difference between both queries.

You can use a query like this:

```
ops$NKHAN@ORA9IR2.WORLD> select /*+ all_rows */
a.user_name, a.sql_text,
b.optimizer_cost
2 from v$open_cursor a, v$sql b
3 where a.address = b.address
4 and a.sid = (select sid from v$mystat where rownum=1)
5 /
```

USER_NAME SQL_TEXT OPTIMIZER_COST

------- ------------------------------- -----------

OPS$NKHAN   BEGIN   DBMS_APPLICATION_INFO.SET_

MODULE(: 0
1,NULL); END;
OPS$NKHAN select /*+ all_rows */ a.user_name, a.sq 122
l_text, b.optimizer_

OPS$NKHAN ALTER SESSION SET NLS_LANGUAGE=
'AMERICA 0
N' NLS_TERRITORY= 'A

OPS$NKHAN SELECT CHAR_VALUE FROM SYSTEM.
PRODUCT_PR 0
IVS WHERE (UPPER('

OPS$NKHAN BEGIN DBMS_OUTPUT.ENABLE(1000000);
END; 0
OPS$NKHAN BEGIN DBMS_OUTPUT.DISABLE; END; 0
OPS$NKHAN SELECT NULL FROM DUAL FOR UPDATE
NOWAIT 0

OPS$NKHAN SELECT ATTRIBUTE,SCOPE,NUMERIC_
VALUE,CHA 0
R_VALUE,DATE_VALUE F

OPS$NKHAN SELECT ATTRIBUTE,SCOPE,NUMERIC_
VALUE,CHA 0
R_VALUE,DATE_VALUE F

OPS$NKHAN SELECT USER FROM DUAL 0
OPS$NKHAN SELECT DECODE('A','A','1','2') FROM DUAL
0

OPS$NKHAN SELECT DECODE('A','A','1','2') FROM DUAL
0

OPS$NKHAN commit 0

OPS$NKHAN select /*+ all_rows */ * from dual 8
OPS$NKHAN select lower(user) || '@' || decode(glob 0
al_name, 'ORACLE8.WO

15 rows selected.

The rows with optimizer cost > 0, those are CBO, and the others
are not. You should not be using CBO on unanalyzed tables, and
as the dictionary is not analyzed, you should not use it there. You
should let the optimizer goal default choose for all 'v$' queries.

☞ QUESTION **55**

Index partition rebuilds query

I want to build the following script using SQL query on oracle dictionary table. It is something like this:

sql> Select 'ALTER INDEX '|| index_name ||' rebuild partition'
.....

e.g.ALTER INDEX <index_name> REBUILD PARTITION <partition_name>

I searched for dictionary tables. I can't find any oracle dictionary table, where I can find the index name along with its partition name.

How can I get the same result?

✎ ANSWER

You can query the table "USER_IND_PARTITIONS" (or ALL_IND_PARTITIONS if you run under another user than the index owner) to get index and partition names.

☞ QUESTION **56**

Oracle server information

What do I need to use to get the following information from my database?

* Mount Point Structure of
Filesystem -blocks Free-%Used-Iused-%Iused-Mounted on

* Database Information â€" Physical Structure of my current database

* v Control Files,v REDO Log Files

* Logical Structure of my current database

* v Invalid Objects with Owner Names

* v Existing Backup Policy

✍ ANSWER

"v$parameter, dba_objects," and "dba_datafiles" would be a good start.

☞ **QUESTION 57**

Batch tuning

What is the purpose of batch tuning in an application?

For example: If the size of database is 1.75TeraByte, then how many tables exist in the database for this data size? I need an approximate figure, if possible.

How many numbers of rows are possible in a table?

✍ **ANSWER**

There is no generalized theory to predict how many tables exist in a database with a size of 175TB. You can login as admin user and issue:

sql>select count(*) from dba_tables;

>> number of rows that is possible in a table.
Virtually unlimited

Batch loading is a process where you load data in a series of steps, and usually it may handle huge volumes of data. This is typically used in a warehouse or in any similar environment.

☞ QUESTION 58

Oracle problem connect by VB application

I'm using VB application to connect oracle db via 'odbc'. Sometimes it works but other times, it raises the error "-2147467259: Oracle error" occurred. The error message could not be retrieved from oracle. I tried to install new mdac and reinstall oracle client, but still results to error.

However, I tried to test connect via odbc testing and sqlplus, and it worked.

The following is the sample syntax:

Provider=MSDAORA.1;User ID=system;Password=manager;
Data Source=database;Persist Security Info=False

os client : windows 2000 pro
oracle client : oracle 8.1.7

os server : sun solaris
db server : oracle 8.1.7
What should I do?

✍ ANSWER

The reason is: [Oracle][ODBC][Ora]ORA-12545: Connect failed because target host or object does not exist.

Whenever this error comes, do check the status of listener

and database on DB server. Both listener and database should be up and running.

The other possible reason is timeout in connectivity. Do check for continuous ping response during the time you are testing your application connectivity with oracle.

☞ QUESTION 59

Archive log getting filled

My archive log file is getting full because my database is hung and then I can't log in the system. How do I resolve the issue? How do I trace an oracle session with a Unix session on HP UNIX? Would the process be different on AIX?

How can I copy my archive logs to another destination?

✍ ANSWER

You can move archive files to another disk to resume database. We archive our archive log files to the tape library, and copy them to another server. So, we have two copies of archive log files.

You should use a tool to alert you when archive files disk is almost full. I use Twisted Nail for Oracle to check for free space on the archive logs disk. I receive an email notification when free space is less than 300 MB.

☞ QUESTION 60

Cursor performance issue

I have the following approach of writing the procedure. Both gave me the same result. I want to know which approach is better in terms of performance.

Take into consideration Parsing, Execution and Other parameters.

The first approach is:
SQL> create or replace procedure proc_comp
2 is
3 begin
4 for i in (select empno,
ename,
job,
sal
from emp
where deptno = 10) loop
5 dbms_output.put_line(i.empno || ' : '||i.ename);
6 end loop;
7 end;
8 /

Procedure created.

The second approach is:
SQL> create or replace procedure proc_comp1
2 is
3 cursor c is
4 select empno,
ename,

job,
sal
5 from emp
6 where deptno = 10;
7 begin
8 for i in c loop
9 dbms_output.put_line(i.empno || ' : '||i.ename);
10 end loop;
11 end;
12 /

✍ ANSWER

The difference is tiny, but the implicit cursor in your first procedure is slightly more efficient than the explicit cursor in your second procedure. I also find the first a bit easier to write, read, and maintain.   If you search for explicit and implicit on "asktom.oracle.com", you will find various discussions where Tom Kyte recommends implicit cursors rather than explicit cursors.

☞ QUESTION 61

Max size of SGA in Oracle 81

What is the maximum size of SGA in a oracle 81 windows 2000 server?

✍ ANSWER

Typically, initially approx 50-60% of your RAM available. Later on, you can change it, depending upon the result in your measures of performance.

☞ QUESTION 62

dbms_stats

I tried to execute the procedure "dbms_stats.get_table_stats", to get the table statistics, but it is giving some errors.

SQL> variable NUMROWS number
SQL> variable NUMBLKS number
SQL> variable AVGRLEN number
SQL> begin
2 SYS.DBMS_STATS.GET_TABLE_STATS('SYSTEM','PROB
LEM',",",",NUMROWS=>:numrows,
3 NUMBLKS=>:numblks,AVGRLEN=>:avgrlen);
4 end;
5 /
begin
*
ERROR at line 1:
ORA-20000: Unable to get values for table PROBLEM
ORA-06512: at "SYS.DBMS_STATS", line 2647
ORA-06512: at line 2
What can use for this?

✍ ANSWER

Please see the demonstration below that first tries to get the table stats without having to gather them first. It then gathers them, and successfully get them. You should also have your tables in another schema, instead of system.

Table and data for testing:

scott@ORA92>   CREATE   TABLE   PROBLEM   (col1
NUMBER)

2 /

Table created.

scott@ORA92> INSERT INTO PROBLEM VALUES (1)

2 /

1 row created.

scott@ORA92> COMMIT

2 /

Commit complete.

– unsuccessful attempt to get table stats:

scott@ORA92> VARIABLE numrows NUMBER

scott@ORA92> VARIABLE numblks NUMBER

scott@ORA92> VARIABLE avgrlen NUMBER

scott@ORA92> SET AUTOPRINT ON

scott@ORA92> BEGIN

2 DBMS_STATS.GET_TABLE_STATS

3   ('SCOTT', 'PROBLEM', NULL, NULL, NULL, :numrows, :
numblks, :avgrlen);

4 END;

5 /

BEGIN

*

ERROR at line 1:

ORA-20000: Unable to get values for table PROBLEM

ORA-06512: at "SYS.DBMS_STATS", line 2582

ORA-06512: at line 2

AVGRLEN

‒‒‒‒‒‒‒‒

NUMBLKS

‒‒‒‒‒‒‒‒

NUMROWS

‒‒‒‒‒‒‒‒

– gather table stats:

scott@ORA92> EXECUTE DBMS_STATS.GATHER_TABLE_

STATS ('SCOTT', 'PROBLEM')
PL/SQL procedure successfully completed.
– now you can get the table stats that have been gathered:
scott@ORA92> VARIABLE numrows NUMBER
scott@ORA92> VARIABLE numblks NUMBER
scott@ORA92> VARIABLE avgrlen NUMBER
scott@ORA92> SET AUTOPRINT ON
scott@ORA92> BEGIN
2 DBMS_STATS.GET_TABLE_STATS
3 ('SCOTT', 'PROBLEM', NULL, NULL, NULL, :numrows, :
numblks, :avgrlen);
4 END;
5 /
PL/SQL procedure successfully completed.
AVGRLEN

3
NUMBLKS

1
NUMROWS

1
scott@ORA92>

☞ QUESTION 63

Rollback segment error in production

I am getting this error on my production. Where can I check for parameters, and how can I resolve this?

ORA-01595: error freeing extent (2) of rollback segment (9))
ORA-01594: attempt to wrap into rollback segment (9) extent (2) which is being freed.

✍ ANSWER

ORA-01595: error freeing extent (1) of rollback segment (7)
ORA-01594: attempt to wrap into rollback segment (7) extent (1) which is being freed

Two factors are necessary for this to happen:

1. A rollback segment has extended beyond optimal.
2. There are two or more transactions sharing the rollback segment at the time of the shrink.

What happens is that the first process gets to the end of an extent, notices the need to shrink, and begins the recursive transaction to do so. The next transaction blunders past the end of that extent before the recursive transaction was committed.

The preferred solution is to have sufficient rollback segments, to eliminate the sharing of rollback segments between processes. Look in "V$RESOURCE_LIMIT" for the high watermark of transactions, that is the number of rollback segments you need. The alternative solution is to raise optimal to reduce the risk of the error.

☞ QUESTION **64**

Tuning question

What are the top 5 tuning techniques when using SQL?

✎ ANSWER

Suggested readings are:

1. Read the Oracle Concepts Guide.

2. Read the Oracle Application Developer Fundamentals Guide.

3. Read the Performance Tuning Guide.

4. Read Effective Oracle By Design by Tom Kyte.

5. Make sure you are using the latest Oracle Release Version.

Other suggestions are:

   a) Use SQL instead of plsql whenever possible.

   b) Use analytic functions.

   c) Use inline views.

   d) Try more than one method and test their plans/stats.

   e) Think about the queries you need to run when creating your tables in the first place.

☞ QUESTION **65**

Analyze table and index

I analyze table and index by issue "analyze table tmp compute statistics for table for all indexed columns;" and got the error: "ORA-00600: internal error code, arguments: [16515], [D], [23], [3031], [7],[0], [], []".

Oracle: 8
Solaris: 2.8

How do I resolve this?

✎ ANSWER

Identify the bug. Delete first the previous statistics, and then collect again. You can start using: "dbms_stats" package.

☞ QUESTION 66

lock_sga parameter

I have oracle 9.0 on windows 2000 server.
My sga size = 470M
pga size = 50M
PHY-MEMORY(RAM) SIZE =1 Gb.

When I configured "lock_sga=true", I got them from memory error when I started the database using that parameter.

I want to configure this parameter in my database. How can I do this?

✍ ANSWER

This is documented as "Oracle BUG 642267".

Problem statement: "LOCK_SGA=TRUE RESULTS IN ORA-27102: OUT OF MEMORY".

Fixed in Product Version: 9.2

Don't use the parameter, try to work around.

For additional information, I find the "lock_sga" parameter very useful on my local Windows XP 10gR1 database.

☞ QUESTION **67**

Check if index is rebuilt or not

How can I determine whether a particular index is rebuilt or not, the size of the index, and what type it was?

How can I know if a user is running an SQL queries which uses an index?

How can I determine what type of index was used?

✍ ANSWER

You can use this to determine if the object was created and not rebuilt:

MYDBA@ORCL > create table t (a number);
Table created.
MYDBA@ORCL > create index tidx on t(a);
Index created.
MYDBA@ORCL > select created from user_objects where object_name = 'TIDX';
CREATED

12-APR-2005 08:44:56
1 row selected.
MYDBA@ORCL > alter index tidx rebuild;
Index altered.
MYDBA@ORCL > select created from user_objects where object_name = 'TIDX';
CREATED

12-APR-2005 08:44:56
1 row selected.
"dba_objects.last_ddl_time", tells you when your last ddl run against your index. It is typically the rebuild.

"dba_segments.blocks", gives the size of the index. If you do analyze compute statistics, you will see other statistics info in "dba_indexes", which also gives you the type of index.

Explain plan will tell you what index the query will use before execution. The right answer to see if the index was used is to do SQL trace dump and use 'tkprof' to look at execution plan. This is the plan that the query used for execution.

Lastly, if you want the real used execution plan, use statspack.

☞ QUESTION **68**

Disk partition strategy

I'm going to install Oracle10g on a Windows 2003 Server.

The Server is provided with a RAID controller and two 146GB SCSI disks, which are in RAID 1 (mirrored).

Do you have any guides to partition the disks for best performance?

✍ **ANSWER**

If you have 2 disks that are mirrored, you end up with one usable disk. How you partition it would not make a big difference. If you want to improve I/O performance, consider adding more disks. Many smaller disks are usually better than a few larger ones.

You may also want to look for a document on the oracle (or otn.oracle) website referring to something called S.A.M.E. Stripe and Mirror Everything.

Basically, if you only have two disks total in mirror, and you don't add anymore, then it doesn't matter what you do at all.

☞ QUESTION 69

the analyze table

I have set analyze to emp table. How can I see that analyzed table?

✍ ANSWER

If you are looking for the times stamp for the date when you analyzed, you can use:

mag@mutation_mutation > select last_analyzed from user_ tables where table_name='EMP';

LAST_ANAL
----
mag@mutation_mutation > ANALYZE TABLE emp COMPUTE STATISTICS;
Table analyzed.
mag@mutation_mutation > select last_analyzed from user_ tables where table_name='EMP';
LAST_ANAL

(date)

☞ QUESTION 70

no_index optimizer hint

After putting "no_index", why did this query used index for
scan? It's the same if I put name of the index in hint.

SELECT /*+ no_index */
NVL (MAX (DUE_DATE), sysdate+10) FROM
CRA.PRECASH WHERE TREATY_NBR = 504 and
ENDORSEMENT_NBR = 0 and TREATY_YR = 2004 AND
SOURCE_SYSTEM_CD = 2
/
Execution Plan
----
0 SELECT STATEMENT Optimizer=CHOOSE (Cost=15
Card=1 Bytes=17)
1 0 SORT (AGGREGATE)
2 1 TABLE ACCESS (BY INDEX ROWID) OF 'PRECASH'
(Cost=15 Card
=1 Bytes=17)

3 2 INDEX (RANGE SCAN) OF 'PRECASH_N2' (NON-
UNIQUE) (Cost=
138 Card=26)

✍ ANSWER

You can read the manuals concerning hints.
The syntax is:

SELECT /*+ no_index (your_table the_index_name)*/

some_column
, another_column
...
FROM your_table
....

In your case, it would be:
SELECT /*+ no_index(PRECASH PRECASH_N2) */

☞ QUESTION **71**

Selecting data out of partition

We have a hash partitioned table, partitioned in columns, and each partition holds only 1 value.

ex: p1=x
p2=y

My question is, would there be a difference in performance if the table is accessed?

select * from table a partition(p1)
vs
select * from table a columna=x

Can you give me the performance of this case?

✍ **ANSWER**

If you are going to be use partitioning, you should go ahead and get use to do an explain plan on queries. Pay particular attention to the 'pstart' and 'pstop' columns towards the right of the explain plan output. It tells you which partitions of the table are accessed in your query. If they have the same value, then you know that CBO knew to hit only one partition, as opposed to the whole table.

Don't mix hash partitioning with list partitioning. List is a set of values that you define when going into specific partitions. Hash is an internal oracle algorithm to "arbitrarily" place values in the different partitions, based on how those values are hashed through an internal algorithm.

In general, I'd suggest against using specific partition names inside of queries. In most cases, that eliminates the transparency that partitions allow. If you change how things are partitioned, then your query is out of luck. Let the CBO make the partition selections for you. Just provide it with enough information (statistics and thoughtful partitioning scheme) so that it can make the appropriate decisions.

☞ QUESTION 72

Server response degrades

We have a server which is Oracle 9.2.0.5 and OS is Windows 2003.

Developers in our company often complain that the server was not responding and it is slow. Then, I have to bounce the DB. It works fine for another 2 to 3 hours, but the same problem occurred again.

There is an average of 15-20 concurrent sessions on the server.

My question is, what could be the loopholes to look for that causes this problem? I don't know what to diagnose exactly.

Previously, the server was fine but recently, we had refreshed it with new dump files that we received from our head office.

How can I fix this?

✍ ANSWER

You should check if the new dump files contain just additional data for existing structures, or if it contains new programs and tables.

You can go back to a back-up before the new dump, and confirm if the problem didn't exist then.

You can also check if you are you running out of memory on the server. Also check if the cursors are closed, and be sure to log people out.

You can also run statspack snapshots of 10 minutes in duration each, every 30 minutes from the time you start the db up to the time you reboot. Do repeatedly with relatively short term snapshot intervals (my numbers are just starting point guesses).

These all would be general things to start with given any unknown performance issue.

☞ QUESTION 73

SQL executed session wise

I want an SQL for "sql_text" executed per session wise. Can you recommend something?

✍ ANSWER

You can try something like this:

```
select sid,
s.username, s.terminal, s.process, s.osuser,
a.sql_text
from sys.v_$session s, sys.v_$sqlarea a
where s.type = 'USER'
and s.sql_address = a.address
and s.sql_hash_value = a.hash_value
/
```

☞ QUESTION 74

ora-02287 sequence not allowed

I am trying to get the top 25 SQL's with the highest 'cpu_time', and insert this into a table. When I added the order by clause, I get "ORA_02287 error". I prefer to do this in the below manner and not with a cursor.

insert into top_sql(topsql_id,username,sql_text,disk_reads,buffer_gets,executions,diskreads_per_exec,buffergets_per_exec,
rows_processed,buffergets_per_row,buffercache_hit_ratio,shareable_memory,sorts,parse_calls,parse_per_exec,loads,cpu_time,
elapsed_time,tune_date)
(select seq_top_id.nextval from dual),
select b.username "User",
a.sql_text "Sql_text",
a.disk_reads "Disk reads",
a.buffer_gets "Buffer gets",
a.executions "Executions",
trunc(a.disk_reads/greatest(a.executions,1)) "Disk reads per execution",
trunc(a.buffer_gets/greatest(a.executions,1)) "Buffer gets per execution",
a.rows_processed " Rows processed",
trunc(a.buffer_gets/greatest(a.rows_processed,1)) "Buffer gets per row",
trunc(a.disk_reads/greatest(buffer_gets,1)*100   )"Buffer cache hit ratio",
a.sharable_mem "Shareable memory",
a.sorts "sorts",
a.Parse_calls "Parse Calls",

trunc(a.parse_calls/greatest(a.executions,1))   "Parse   calls
per execution",
a.Loads "Loads",
a.Cpu_time "Cpu_time",
a.elapsed_time "Elasped_time",
sysdate
from sys.v_$sql a,
sys.all_users b
where a.parsing_user_id=b.user_id and
b.username not in ('SYS','SYSTEM')
and rownum < 26
order by cpu_time desc

✍ ANSWER

It's probably just a syntax error. Try:

insert   into   top_sql(topsql_id,username,sql_text,disk_
reads,buffer_gets,executions,diskreads_per_
exec,buffergets_per_exec,
rows_processed,buffergets_per_row,buffercache_hit_
ratio,shareable_memory,sorts,parse_calls,parse_per_
exec,loads,cpu_time,
elapsed_time,tune_date)
select seq_top_id.nextval, b.username "User",

☞ QUESTION 75

Performance tuning a query

I tried to tune this query but it took me 10 minutes to execute it. How can I improve the response time of this query? My version is 9.2.0.5 and O.S. win 2003.

Query:

SELECT /*+FIRST_ROWS*/

(SELECT /*+FIRST_ROWS*/
I.CUSTOMER_ID
from ARV_SOP_ACTION_ITEM AI,
ARV_SOP_RECIPIENT_INFO RI,
AV_ANY_INDIVIDUAL I
where AI.WORKSHEET_ID = W.WORKSHEET_ID and
AI.DELIVERABLE_CD = 12007 and
AI.DELIVERY_METHOD_CD != 13014 and
AI.ACTION_ITEM_STATUS_CD in (38002, 38003) and
AI.RECIPIENT_INFO_ID = RI.RECIPIENT_INFO_ID and
RI.RECIPIENT_ID = I.INDIVIDUAL_ID and RI.RECIPIENT_
ID is not null) CustomerNoOfPriRecp,

(SELECT NVL((SELECT /*+FIRST_ROWS*/
RI.RECIPIENT_NAME
from ARV_SOP_ACTION_ITEM AI, ARV_SOP_RECIPIENT_
INFO RI
where AI.WORKSHEET_ID = W.WORKSHEET_ID and
AI.RECIPIENT_INFO_ID = RI.RECIPIENT_INFO_ID and
AI.DELIVERABLE_CD = 12007 and
AI.DELIVERY_METHOD_CD != 13014 and
AI.ACTION_ITEM_STATUS_CD in (38002, 38003)),

' -- ')
FROM DUAL) PrimaryRecpName,

(SELECT NVL((SELECT /*+FIRST_ROWS*/
RI.PHONE
from ARV_SOP_ACTION_ITEM AI, ARV_SOP_RECIPIENT_
INFO RI
where AI.WORKSHEET_ID = W.WORKSHEET_ID and
AI.RECIPIENT_INFO_ID = RI.RECIPIENT_INFO_ID and
AI.DELIVERABLE_CD = 12007 and
AI.DELIVERY_METHOD_CD != 13014 and
AI.ACTION_ITEM_STATUS_CD in (38002, 38003)),
' -- ')
FROM DUAL) PrimaryRecpPhone,

(SELECT /*+FIRST_ROWS*/
I.CUSTOMER_ID
from ARV_SOP_ACTION_ITEM AI,
ARV_SOP_RECIPIENT_INFO RI,
AV_ANY_INDIVIDUAL I
where AI.WORKSHEET_ID = W.WORKSHEET_ID and
AI.DELIVERABLE_CD = 12008 and
AI.DELIVERY_METHOD_CD not in (13016, 13017) and
AI.ACTION_ITEM_STATUS_CD = 38002 and
AI.RECIPIENT_INFO_ID = RI.RECIPIENT_INFO_ID and
RI.RECIPIENT_ID = I.INDIVIDUAL_ID and RI.RECIPIENT_
ID is not null and
ROWNUM = 1) CCRecipientCustomerNo,

(SELECT NVL((SELECT /*+FIRST_ROWS*/
RI.RECIPIENT_NAME
from ARV_SOP_ACTION_ITEM AI, ARV_SOP_RECIPIENT_
INFO RI
where AI.WORKSHEET_ID = W.WORKSHEET_ID and
AI.RECIPIENT_INFO_ID = RI.RECIPIENT_INFO_ID and

AI.DELIVERABLE_CD = 12008 and
AI.ACTION_ITEM_STATUS_CD = 38002 and
AI.DELIVERY_METHOD_CD not in (13016, 13017) and
ROWNUM = 1),
' – ')
FROM DUAL) CCRecpName,

(SELECT NVL((SELECT /*+FIRST_ROWS*/
RI.PHONE
from ARV_SOP_ACTION_ITEM AI, ARV_SOP_RECIPIENT_
INFO RI
where AI.WORKSHEET_ID = W.WORKSHEET_ID and
AI.RECIPIENT_INFO_ID = RI.RECIPIENT_INFO_ID and
AI.DELIVERABLE_CD = 12008 and
AI.ACTION_ITEM_STATUS_CD = 38002 and
AI.DELIVERY_METHOD_CD not in (13016, 13017) and
ROWNUM = 1),
' – ')
FROM DUAL) CCRecpPhone,

(SELECT /*+FIRST_ROWS*/
nvl(trim(E.TRUE_NAME), '–')
from ARV_BUSINESS_NAME BN, ARV_ENTITY E
where   BN.BUS_NAME_ID   =   W.BUS_NAME_ID   and
E.ENTITY_ID = BN.ENTITY_ID) EntityName,

(SELECT /*+FIRST_ROWS*/
nvl(trim(J.JURIS_NAME), '–')
from ARV_JURISDICTION J
where J.JURIS_ID = W.REP_JURIS_ID) JurisWhereProcess
WasServed,

(SELECT /*+FIRST_ROWS*/
ST.NAME
from AV_SERVICE_TEAM ST

where ST.SERVICE_TEAM_ID = W.OWNING_TEAM_ID)
TeamReceivingProcess,

(SELECT /*+FIRST_ROWS*/
trim(STM.FIRST_NAME) || ' ' || trim(STM.LAST_NAME)
from AV_SERVICE_TEAM_MEMBER STM
where   W.ASSIGNED_TO   =   STM.SERVICE_TEAM_
MEMBER_ID) AssignedTo,

W.WORKSHEET_ID LogNumber,

(SELECT /*+FIRST_ROWS*/
count(*)
from ARV_SOP_CASE SC
where SC.WORKSHEET_ID = W.WORKSHEET_ID and
SC.CASE_TYPE = 'S') NumberOfCases,

W.RECEIVED_DATE DateOfSOPReceipt,

(SELECT /*+FIRST_ROWS*/
RM.RECEIVED_METHOD
from ARV_SOP_RECEIVED_METHOD RM
where RM.RECEIVED_METHOD_CD = W.RECEIVED_
METHOD_CD) MethodOfReceipt,

nvl((SELECT /*+FIRST_ROWS*/
C.PLAINTIFF
from ARV_SOP_CASE C
where   C.CASE_ID   =   ARFN_GET_SOP_CASE_ID(W.
WORKSHEET_ID)),
'--') Plaintiff,

W.NATURE_OF_ACTION NatureOfAction,

(SELECT /*+FIRST_ROWS*/

LT.lawsuit_type
from ARV_LAWSUIT_TYPE LT
where   LT.lawsuit_type_cd   =   W.LAWSUIT_TYPE_CD)
LawSuitType,

(SELECT /*+FIRST_ROWS*/
LST.LAWSUIT_SUBTYPE
from ARV_LAWSUIT_SUBTYPE LST
where   LST.LAWSUIT_SUBTYPE_CD   =   W.LAWSUIT_
SUBTYPE_CD) LawSuitSubType,

W.DOCUMENT_TYPE DocumentType,

W.ANSWER_DATE AnswerDate,

W.COURT_NAME CourtName,

(SELECT NVL((SELECT /*+FIRST_ROWS*/
'Y'
from ARV_SOP_ACTION_ITEM AI
where AI.WORKSHEET_ID = W.WORKSHEET_ID and
AI.DELIVERY_METHOD_CD = 13014 and
AI.ACTION_ITEM_STATUS_CD = 38002),
'N')
FROM DUAL) ISOPPosted,

(SELECT NVL((SELECT /*+FIRST_ROWS*/
'Y'
from ARV_SOP_ACTION_ITEM AI, ARV_SOP_RECIPIENT_
INFO RI
where AI.WORKSHEET_ID = W.WORKSHEET_ID and
AI.RECIPIENT_INFO_ID = RI.RECIPIENT_INFO_ID and
AI.DELIVERABLE_CD = 12008 and
AI.DELIVERY_METHOD_CD = 13016 and
AI.ACTION_ITEM_STATUS_CD = 38008 and

RI.RECIPIENT_ID in
(SELECT /*+FIRST_ROWS*/
RI.RECIPIENT_ID
from ARV_SOP_ACTION_ITEM AI, ARV_SOP_RECIPIENT_
INFO RI
where AI.WORKSHEET_ID = W.WORKSHEET_ID and
AI.RECIPIENT_INFO_ID = RI.RECIPIENT_INFO_ID and
AI.DELIVERABLE_CD = 12007 and
AI.DELIVERY_METHOD_CD != 13014 and
AI.ACTION_ITEM_STATUS_CD in (38002, 38003)) and
rownum = 1),
'N')
from dual) EmailSentToPrimaryRecipient,

(SELECT NVL((SELECT /*+FIRST_ROWS*/
'Y'
from ARV_SOP_ACTION_ITEM AI, ARV_SOP_RECIPIENT_
INFO RI
where AI.WORKSHEET_ID = W.WORKSHEET_ID and
AI.RECIPIENT_INFO_ID = RI.RECIPIENT_INFO_ID and
AI.DELIVERABLE_CD = 12008 and
AI.DELIVERY_METHOD_CD = 13016 and
AI.ACTION_ITEM_STATUS_CD = 38008 and
RI.RECIPIENT_ID in
(SELECT /*+FIRST_ROWS*/
RI.RECIPIENT_ID
from ARV_SOP_ACTION_ITEM AI, ARV_SOP_RECIPIENT_
INFO RI
where AI.WORKSHEET_ID = W.WORKSHEET_ID and
AI.RECIPIENT_INFO_ID = RI.RECIPIENT_INFO_ID and
AI.DELIVERABLE_CD = 12008 and
AI.DELIVERY_METHOD_CD in
(13010, 13018, 13019, 13020) and
AI.ACTION_ITEM_STATUS_CD = 38002) and ROWNUM =
1),

'N')
from dual) EmailSentToCCRecipient,

(SELECT NVL((SELECT /*+FIRST_ROWS*/
DM.DELIVERY_METHOD
from ARV_SOP_ACTION_ITEM AI, ARV_DI_DELIVERY_
METHOD DM
where AI.WORKSHEET_ID = W.WORKSHEET_ID and
AI.DELIVERY_METHOD_CD = DM.DELIVERY_METHOD_
CD and
AI.DELIVERABLE_CD = 12007 and
AI.DELIVERY_METHOD_CD != 13014 and
AI.ACTION_ITEM_STATUS_CD in (38002, 38003)),
' -- ')
FROM DUAL) MethodOfService,

(SELECT NVL((SELECT /*+FIRST_ROWS*/
DM.DELIVERY_METHOD
from ARV_SOP_ACTION_ITEM AI, ARV_DI_DELIVERY_
METHOD DM
where AI.WORKSHEET_ID = W.WORKSHEET_ID and
AI.DELIVERY_METHOD_CD = DM.DELIVERY_METHOD_
CD and
AI.DELIVERY_METHOD_CD in (13010, 13018, 13019, 13020)
and
AI.DELIVERABLE_CD = 12008 and
AI.ACTION_ITEM_STATUS_CD in (38002) and ROWNUM =
1),
' -- ')
FROM DUAL) MethodOfServiceForCCRecipient,

/* (SELECT
NVL((SELECT *+FIRST_ROWS*\
DM.DELIVERY_METHOD
from

ARV_SOP_ACTION_ITEM AI,
ARV_DI_DELIVERY_METHOD DM
where
AI.WORKSHEET_ID = W.WORKSHEET_ID and
AI.DELIVERY_METHOD_CD = DM.DELIVERY_METHOD_
CD and
AI.DELIVERY_METHOD_CD in (13015) and
AI.DELIVERABLE_CD = 12008 and
AI.ACTION_ITEM_STATUS_CD in (38002) and
ROWNUM = 1
),' – ')
FROM DUAL) AddActionItemInfo, */

/*('DELIVERABLE - ' ||
(SELECT
D.DELIVERABLE_NAME
from
ARV_DI_DELIVERABLE D
where
D.DELIVERABLE_CD = AI.DELIVERABLE_CD)
|| ' ' || ', DELIVERY METHOD - ' ||
(SELECT
DM.DELIVERY_METHOD
from
ARV_DI_DELIVERY_METHOD DM
where dm.delivery_method_cd = AI.DELIVERY_METHOD_
CD)
|| ' ' || ', ACTION ITEM STATUS - ' ||
(SELECT
AIS.ACTION_ITEM_STATUS
from
ARV_ACTION_ITEM_STATUS AIS
where
AIS.ACTION_ITEM_STATUS_CD = AI.ACTION_ITEM_
STATUS_CD)) AddActionItemInfo, */

(SELECT /*+FIRST_ROWS*/
SC.COMMENTS
from ARV_SOP_COMMENT SC
where SC.WORKSHEET_ID = W.WORKSHEET_ID and
SC.COMMENT_TYPE = 'R') WorksheetRemarks,

(SELECT NVL((SELECT /*+FIRST_ROWS*/
'Y'
from ARV_SOP_ACTION_ITEM AI, ARV_SOP_RECIPIENT_
INFO RI
where AI.WORKSHEET_ID = W.WORKSHEET_ID and
AI.RECIPIENT_INFO_ID = RI.RECIPIENT_INFO_ID and
AI.DELIVERY_METHOD_CD = 13015 and
AI.DELIVERABLE_CD = 12006 and
AI.ACTION_ITEM_STATUS_CD = 38002 and
RI.RECIPIENT_ID in
(SELECT /*+FIRST_ROWS*/
RI.RECIPIENT_ID
from ARV_SOP_ACTION_ITEM AI, ARV_SOP_RECIPIENT_
INFO RI
where AI.WORKSHEET_ID = W.WORKSHEET_ID and
AI.RECIPIENT_INFO_ID = RI.RECIPIENT_INFO_ID and
AI.DELIVERABLE_CD = 12007 and
AI.DELIVERY_METHOD_CD != 13014 and
AI.ACTION_ITEM_STATUS_CD in (38002, 38003)) and
ROWNUM = 1),
'N')
FROM DUAL) PhoneActionSentToPrimaryRecp,

(SELECT NVL((SELECT /*+FIRST_ROWS*/
'Y'
from ARV_SOP_ACTION_ITEM AI, ARV_SOP_RECIPIENT_
INFO RI
where AI.WORKSHEET_ID = W.WORKSHEET_ID and
AI.RECIPIENT_INFO_ID = RI.RECIPIENT_INFO_ID and

AI.DELIVERY_METHOD_CD = 13015 and
AI.DELIVERABLE_CD = 12006 and
AI.ACTION_ITEM_STATUS_CD = 38002 and
RI.RECIPIENT_ID in
(SELECT /*+FIRST_ROWS*/
RI.RECIPIENT_ID
from ARV_SOP_ACTION_ITEM AI, ARV_SOP_RECIPIENT_
INFO RI
where AI.WORKSHEET_ID = W.WORKSHEET_ID and
AI.RECIPIENT_INFO_ID = RI.RECIPIENT_INFO_ID and
AI.DELIVERABLE_CD = 12008 and
AI.DELIVERY_METHOD_CD in
(13010, 13018, 13019, 13020) and
AI.ACTION_ITEM_STATUS_CD = 38002) and ROWNUM =
1),
'N')
FROM DUAL) PhoneActionSentToCCRecp,

(SELECT decode((SELECT /*+FIRST_ROWS*/
AM.AFFL_ID
from arv_affl_membership AM, ARV_BUSINESS_NAME BN
where BN.BUS_NAME_ID = W.BUS_NAME_ID and
AM.ENTITY_ID = BN.ENTITY_ID),
null,
(SELECT /*+FIRST_ROWS*/
count(*)
from ARV_REPRESENTATION R, ARV_BUSINESS_NAME
BN
where R.ENTITY_ID = BN.ENTITY_ID and
BN.BUS_NAME_ID = W.BUS_NAME_ID),
(SELECT /*+FIRST_ROWS*/
count(*)
fromARV_REPRESENTATIONR,ARV_AFFL_MEMBERSHIP
AM
where R.ENTITY_ID = AM.ENTITY_ID and

AM.AFFL_ID =
(SELECT /*+FIRST_ROWS*/
AM.AFFL_ID
from ARV_AFFL_MEMBERSHIP AM, ARV_BUSINESS_
NAME BN
where BN.BUS_NAME_ID = W.BUS_NAME_ID and
AM.ENTITY_ID = BN.ENTITY_ID)))
from DUAL) RepUnitsforRecpEntity

from ARV_SOP_WORKSHEET W
where
–W.WORKSHEET_ID = 510000015
trunc(W.CREATED_DATE) = '25-JUN-1994'

Expalin Plan:-

SELECT STATEMENT, GOAL = HINT: FIRST_ROWS 40687
65246 15202318
NESTED LOOPS 4 9 513
NESTED LOOPS 3 1 40
TABLE ACCESS BY INDEX ROWID ARROW TSOP_ACTION_
ITEM 2 1 28
INDEX RANGE SCAN ARROW SOP_ACTION_ITEM_
WDDA_PNDX 2 1
TABLE ACCESS BY INDEX ROWID ARROW TSOP_
RECIPIENT_INFO 2 1 12
INDEX UNIQUE SCAN ARROW TSOP_RECIPIENT_INFO_
PK 1
VIEW GDS AV_ANY_INDIVIDUAL 2 9 153
UNION-ALL PARTITION
NESTED LOOPS 3 1 38
TABLE ACCESS BY INDEX ROWID GDS TINDIVIDUAL_
KEYS 2 1 27
INDEX UNIQUE SCAN GDS TINDIVIDUAL_KEYS_PK 2 1
INDEX RANGE SCAN GDS TCUSTOMER_KEYS_UX3 1 1

11
NESTED LOOPS 6 1 61
NESTED LOOPS 5 1 50
NESTED LOOPS 4 1 38
NESTED LOOPS 3 1 32
TABLE ACCESS BY INDEX ROWID GDS TINDIVIDUAL_
KEYS 2 1 27
INDEX UNIQUE SCAN GDS TINDIVIDUAL_KEYS_PK 2 1
INDEX UNIQUE SCAN JDEDTA F0101_PK 1 5
INDEX UNIQUE SCAN JDEDTA F0111_PK 1 6
INDEX RANGE SCAN JDEDTA F0150_UX1 1 1 12
INDEX RANGE SCAN GDS TCUSTOMER_KEYS_UX3 1 1
11
TABLE ACCESS FULL SYS DUAL 11 8168
TABLE ACCESS FULL SYS DUAL 11 8168
COUNT STOPKEY
NESTED LOOPS 4 4 228
NESTED LOOPS 3 1 40
TABLE ACCESS BY INDEX ROWID ARROW TSOP_ACTION_
ITEM 2 1 28
INDEX RANGE SCAN ARROW SOP_ACTION_ITEM_
WDDA_PNDX 2 1
TABLE ACCESS BY INDEX ROWID ARROW TSOP_
RECIPIENT_INFO 2 1 12
INDEX UNIQUE SCAN ARROW TSOP_RECIPIENT_INFO_
PK 1
VIEW GDS AV_ANY_INDIVIDUAL 2 9 153
UNION-ALL PARTITION
NESTED LOOPS 3 1 38
TABLE ACCESS BY INDEX ROWID GDS TINDIVIDUAL_
KEYS 2 1 27
INDEX UNIQUE SCAN GDS TINDIVIDUAL_KEYS_PK 2 1
INDEX RANGE SCAN GDS TCUSTOMER_KEYS_UX3 1 1
11
NESTED LOOPS 6 1 61

NESTED LOOPS 5 1 50
NESTED LOOPS 4 1 38
NESTED LOOPS 3 1 32
TABLE ACCESS BY INDEX ROWID GDS TINDIVIDUAL_
KEYS 2 1 27
INDEX UNIQUE SCAN GDS TINDIVIDUAL_KEYS_PK 2 1
INDEX UNIQUE SCAN JDEDTA F0101_PK 1 5
INDEX UNIQUE SCAN JDEDTA F0111_PK 1 6
INDEX RANGE SCAN JDEDTA F0150_UX1 1 1 12
INDEX RANGE SCAN GDS TCUSTOMER_KEYS_UX3 1 1
11
TABLE ACCESS FULL SYS DUAL 11 8168
TABLE ACCESS FULL SYS DUAL 11 8168
NESTED LOOPS 3 1 50
TABLE ACCESS BY INDEX ROWID ARROW TBUSINESS_
NAME 2 1 14
INDEX UNIQUE SCAN ARROW BUSINESS_NAME_PK 2 1
TABLE ACCESS BY INDEX ROWID ARROW TENTITY 2 1
36
INDEX UNIQUE SCAN ARROW ENTITY_PK 1
FILTER
TABLE ACCESS BY INDEX ROWID GDS TJURISDICTION_
KEYS 2 1 66
INDEX UNIQUE SCAN GDS TJURISDICTION_KEYS_PK 1
1
NESTED LOOPS OUTER 35 51 4539
NESTED LOOPS 15 51 4029
NESTED LOOPS 5 51 2295
NESTED LOOPS 4 1 29
NESTED LOOPS 3 1 20
TABLE   ACCESS   BY   INDEX   ROWID   GDS
TORGANIZATIONAL_UNIT_KEYS 2 1 10
INDEX UNIQUE SCAN GDS TORGANIZATIONAL_UNIT_
KEYS_PK 1 1
TABLE ACCESS BY INDEX ROWID JDEDTA F0101 2 1 10

INDEX UNIQUE SCAN JDEDTA F0101_PK 1
INDEX UNIQUE SCAN JDEDTA F0116_PK 1 9
INDEX RANGE SCAN JDEDTA F0005_PK 1 51 816
INDEX RANGE SCAN JDEDTA F550101_X2 1 1 34
TABLE ACCESS BY INDEX ROWID JDEDTA F0150 2 1 10
INDEX RANGE SCAN JDEDTA F0150_UX1 1 1
NESTED LOOPS 12 1 156
NESTED LOOPS 11 1 151
NESTED LOOPS OUTER 10 1 142
NESTED LOOPS 9 1 132
NESTED LOOPS 8 1 116
NESTED LOOPS 7 1 106
NESTED LOOPS 6 1 96
NESTED LOOPS 5 1 86
NESTED LOOPS 4 1 70
NESTED LOOPS 3 1 15
TABLE ACCESS BY INDEX ROWID GDS TEMPLOYEE_
KEYS 2 1 7
INDEX UNIQUE SCAN GDS TEMPLOYEE_KEYS_PK 1 1
TABLE ACCESS BY INDEX ROWID JDEDTA F0101 2 1 8
INDEX UNIQUE SCAN JDEDTA F0101_PK 1
TABLE ACCESS BY INDEX ROWID JDEDTA F0111 2 1 55
INDEX RANGE SCAN JDEDTA F0111_PK 1 1
TABLE ACCESS BY INDEX ROWID JDEDTA F0150 2 1 16
INDEX RANGE SCAN JDEDTA F0150_UX1 1 1
INDEX RANGE SCAN GDS TORGANIZATIONAL_UNIT_
KEYS_UX1 1 1 10
TABLE   ACCESS   BY   INDEX   ROWID   GDS
TORGANIZATIONAL_UNIT_KEYS 2 1 10
INDEX UNIQUE SCAN GDS TORGANIZATIONAL_UNIT_
KEYS_PK 1
TABLE ACCESS BY INDEX ROWID JDEDTA F0101 2 1 10
INDEX UNIQUE SCAN JDEDTA F0101_PK 1
INDEX RANGE SCAN JDEDTA F0005_PK 1 1 16
TABLE ACCESS BY INDEX ROWID JDEDTA F0150 2 1 10

INDEX RANGE SCAN JDEDTA F0150_UX1 1 1
INDEX UNIQUE SCAN JDEDTA F0116_PK 1 9
INDEX RANGE SCAN JDEDTA F550101_PK 1 1 5
SORT AGGREGATE 1 6
INDEX RANGE SCAN ARROW SOP_CASE_COMPOSE_
NUM_PNDX 3 3 18
TABLE ACCESS BY INDEX ROWID ARROW TLOOKUP 2 1
25
INDEX UNIQUE SCAN ARROW LOOKUP_PK 1
TABLE ACCESS BY INDEX ROWID ARROW TSOP_CASE 2
1 36
INDEX UNIQUE SCAN ARROW TSOP_CASE_PK 2 1
TABLE ACCESS BY INDEX ROWID ARROW TLOOKUP 2 1
25
INDEX UNIQUE SCAN ARROW LOOKUP_PK 1
TABLE ACCESS BY INDEX ROWID ARROW TLOOKUP 2 1
25
INDEX UNIQUE SCAN ARROW LOOKUP_PK 1
TABLE ACCESS FULL SYS DUAL 11 8168
TABLE ACCESS FULL SYS DUAL 11 8168
TABLE ACCESS FULL SYS DUAL 11 8168
TABLE ACCESS FULL SYS DUAL 11 8168
TABLE ACCESS FULL SYS DUAL 11 8168
TABLE ACCESS BY INDEX ROWID ARROW TSOP_
COMMENT 2 1 69
INDEX RANGE SCAN ARROW SOP_COMMENT_WSID_
PNDX 1 2
TABLE ACCESS FULL SYS DUAL 11 8168
TABLE ACCESS FULL SYS DUAL 11 8168
TABLE ACCESS FULL SYS DUAL 11 8168
TABLE ACCESS FULL ARROW TSOP_WORKSHEET 40687
65246 15202318

✍ ANSWER

If you just want to replace a value when it is null, then you do not need the outer query. However, if you want to supply a value when the inner query does not return a row at all, then you will need the outer query. You can try to execute each sub query separately and find out which is taking the longest time. Then, examine that sub query in more detail to see what can be done. I noticed that your last where clause relies on an implicit date conversion, which is generally a bad idea because it will cause the query to fail if the "nls_date_format" does not match.

Another thing, you might try to move the inline views in the select clause to the from clause without the calls to dual and nvl, then the outer joining them and putting the nvl functions in the outer select. So, instead of:

SELECT /*+FIRST_ROWS*/
(SELECT /*+FIRST_ROWS*/
I.CUSTOMER_ID
FROMARV_SOP_ACTION_ITEMAI,ARV_SOP_RECIPIENT_
INFO RI, AV_ANY_INDIVIDUAL I
WHERE AI.WORKSHEET_ID = W.WORKSHEET_ID
AND AI.DELIVERABLE_CD = 12007
AND AI.DELIVERY_METHOD_CD != 13014
AND AI.ACTION_ITEM_STATUS_CD in (38002, 38003)
AND AI.RECIPIENT_INFO_ID = RI.RECIPIENT_INFO_ID
AND RI.RECIPIENT_ID = I.INDIVIDUAL_ID
AND RI.RECIPIENT_ID is not null) CustomerNoOfPriRecp,
(SELECT NVL ((SELECT /*+FIRST_ROWS*/
RI.RECIPIENT_NAME
FROM   ARV_SOP_ACTION_ITEM   AI,   ARV_SOP_
RECIPIENT_INFO RI

```
WHERE AI.WORKSHEET_ID = W.WORKSHEET_ID
AND AI.RECIPIENT_INFO_ID = RI.RECIPIENT_INFO_ID
AND AI.DELIVERABLE_CD = 12007
AND AI.DELIVERY_METHOD_CD != 13014
AND AI.ACTION_ITEM_STATUS_CD in (38002, 38003)), ' -
- ')
FROM DUAL) PrimaryRecpName,
...
FROM ARV_SOP_WORKSHEET W
WHERE trunc (W.CREATED_DATE) = '25-JUN-1994'
/
```

you would have:
```
SELECT /*+FIRST_ROWS*/
CustomerNoOfPriRecp.customer_id                          as
CustomerNoOfPriRecp,
NVL      (PrimaryRecpName.recipient_name,      '–')      as
PrimaryRecpName
...
FROM ARV_SOP_WORKSHEET W,
(SELECT I.CUSTOMER_ID, ai.worksheet_id
FROM ARV_SOP_ACTION_ITEM AI, ARV_SOP_RECIPIENT_
INFO RI, AV_ANY_INDIVIDUAL I
WHERE AI.DELIVERABLE_CD = 12007
AND AI.DELIVERY_METHOD_CD != 13014
AND AI.ACTION_ITEM_STATUS_CD in (38002, 38003)
AND AI.RECIPIENT_INFO_ID = RI.RECIPIENT_INFO_ID
AND RI.RECIPIENT_ID = I.INDIVIDUAL_ID
AND RI.RECIPIENT_ID is not null) CustomerNoOfPriRecp,
(SELECT RI.RECIPIENT_NAME, ai.worksheet_id
FROM      ARV_SOP_ACTION_ITEM      AI,      ARV_SOP_
RECIPIENT_INFO RI
WHERE AI.RECIPIENT_INFO_ID = RI.RECIPIENT_INFO_
ID
AND AI.DELIVERABLE_CD = 12007
```

AND AI.DELIVERY_METHOD_CD != 13014
AND AI.ACTION_ITEM_STATUS_CD in (38002, 38003))
PrimaryRecpName,
...
WHERE trunc (W.CREATED_DATE) = to_date ('25-JUN-1994', 'dd-MON-yyyy')
AND w.worksheeet_id = CustomerNoOfPriRecp.worksheet_id
AND w.worksheet_id = PrimaryRecpName.worksheet_id (+)
/

It allows the tables to join directly and eliminate the calls to the dual table. It still allows for a value substitution when the sub query does not produce a row.

I also noticed that you have a number of sub queries that select from the same tables, with different filtering conditions. You could eliminate some duplication by using with clause or sub query factoring clause. So, instead of:

SELECT (SELECT some_column
FROM   ARV_SOP_ACTION_ITEM   AI,   ARV_SOP_RECIPIENT_INFO RI
WHERE AI.RECIPIENT_INFO_ID = RI.RECIPIENT_INFO_ID
AND some_filter_conditions),
(SELECT some_other_column
FROM   ARV_SOP_ACTION_ITEM   AI,   ARV_SOP_RECIPIENT_INFO RI
WHERE AI.RECIPIENT_INFO_ID = RI.RECIPIENT_INFO_ID
AND some_other_filter_conditions)

you could have:
WITH repeating_query AS
(SELECT *

FROM   ARV_SOP_ACTION_ITEM   AI,   ARV_SOP_
RECIPIENT_INFO RI
WHERE AI.RECIPIENT_INFO_ID = RI.RECIPIENT_INFO_ID)
SELECT (SELECT some_column
FROM repeating_query
WHERE some_other_filter_conditions),
(SELECT some_other_column
FROM repeating_query
WHERE some_filter_conditions)

☞ QUESTION 76

Index and changing selected columns

I have a join for three tables which are joined by primary keys. When I use a particular column in select clause, the index on "Ship_status" is used. When I give three or more columns, then the full table scan is then made for "RMA_ LINES_EXT" table. No modification was done in the where clause. I have an impression that if I change where clause, then only the execution plan should change, but changing columns in select also changes it.

select /*+ INDEX (EBCLIENT.RMA_LINES_EXT RMA_ LINES_EXT_SS) */
h.returnaction RETURN_TYPE ,
a.QTY_TO_SHIP from ebdb.ralinehistory h, ebclient.rma_ lines_ext a,
ebclient.rmalinetable r
where a.rma_line_id = h.linekey
and r.rma_line_id = a.rma_line_id
and ship_status = 'Ready'

✍ ANSWER

It's not necessary that the optimizer will choose indexes based upon your where clauses. Basically, when a select includes columns which can be read directly from the index rather than reading the table, the optimizer will do it.

cdl_domain@DEEPRED> create table temp as select object_ id , owner , object_name

2 from all_objects
Table created.

cdl_domain@DEEPRED> create index idx_temp_name on temp(object_name);

Index created.

cdl_domain@DEEPRED>
cdl_domain@DEEPRED> analyze table temp
2 compute statistics
3 for table
4 for all indexes
5 for all indexed columns
6 /

Table analyzed.

cdl_domain@DEEPRED> set autot traceonly

cdl_domain@DEEPRED> select object_name from temp;

26490 rows selected.

Execution Plan
```
---------------------------------------------
```
0   SELECT   STATEMENT   Optimizer=CHOOSE   (Cost=14
Card=26490 Bytes=
1 0 INDEX (FAST FULL SCAN) OF 'IDX_TEMP_NAME'
(NON-UNIQUE) (Co

Statistics
```
---------------------------------------------
```
0 recursive calls
0 db block gets

1899 consistent gets
0 physical reads
0 redo size
707192 bytes sent via SQL*Net to client
19914 bytes received via SQL*Net from client
1767 SQL*Net roundtrips to/from client
0 sorts (memory)
0 sorts (disk)
26490 rows processed

As you can see, there is no where clause in the select statement. The optimizer chooses the index because it's cheaper to read through the index rather than the whole table.

☞ QUESTION 77

Full table scan with varying consistence

I have a table with 50,000 rows. When I perform a query which requires 5% of the table, less consistent gets are used than a query requiring 100% of the table.

The consistent gets rise steadily as the row selectivity increases from 5 to 100%, so it is not a freak occurrence.

I thought consistent gets were used when reading the table, and a full table scans needs to read the whole table, which means that there should be no difference.

Can anyone tell me why this is happening?

Here are my explain plans:

1 - 5%
select /*+ Full(biggertable50000) */* from biggertable50000 where ID <=2500;

2500 rows selected.

Execution Plan
----
0 SELECT STATEMENT Optimizer=CHOOSE (Cost=371 Card=3895 Bytes=
334970)

1 0 TABLE ACCESS (FULL) OF 'BIGGERTABLE50000' (Cost=371 Card=3
895 Bytes=334970)

Statistics

---

144 recursive calls
7 db block gets
4026 consistent gets
3860 physical reads
0 redo size
60704 bytes sent via SQL*Net to client
11693 bytes received via SQL*Net from client
169 SQL*Net roundtrips to/from client
5 sorts (memory)
0 sorts (disk)
2500 rows processed

Elapsed: 00:00:13.09

 2 - 100%
select /*+ Full(biggertable50000) */* from biggertable50000
where ID <=50000;

50000 rows selected.

 Execution Plan

---

0 SELECT STATEMENT Optimizer=CHOOSE (Cost=371
Card=3895 Bytes=
334970)

1 0 TABLE ACCESS (FULL) OF 'BIGGERTABLE50000'
(Cost=371 Card=3
895 Bytes=334970)

Statistics

---

0 recursive calls

6 db block gets
6926 consistent gets
3819 physical reads
0 redo size
1249741 bytes sent via SQL*Net to client
230218 bytes received via SQL*Net from client
3336 SQL*Net roundtrips to/from client
1 sorts (memory)
0 sorts (disk)
50000 rows processed

Elapsed: 00:03:57.09

✍ Answer

Consistent gets is the number of accesses made to the buffer
cache to retrieve data in a consistent mode. Most accesses
are done with the "consistent get" mechanism, which uses
the SCN (System Change Number) to ensure the data being
read has not changed since the query was started.

The more data you read from cache, the higher consistent
gets would be.

☞ QUESTION 78

Parallel hint question

I'm currently working on 8.1.7 version of Oracle.

I came across a document which states that: " parallel hint works fine when they have multiple processors which will make the operation run even faster, and the table should be striped".

It also stated that the degree of parallelism and the number of parallel servers were sourced from the parameters specified in the "INIT.ORA file".

If I want to use this a hint for DML operation in my stored procedure, how will I know the following:

1) Degree of Parallelism or number of query servers for the table?
2) Number of Oracle parallel server instances to split the query across?
3) Whether my data files is striped across multiple disks or not?

Are there any dictionary tables which can be queried?

✎ ANSWER

Unless you are operating on an extremely high transaction system, I would not worry about putting parallel hints on the query. Just apply the appropriate parameters in the "INIT" file and Oracle will decide to use the parallel capability.

Worry more about how long Oracle is going to support 8i version.

Another suggestion is to do the following:

1. Include parallel hint in the queries written in procedures/ function.
2. Alter the tables which are used in functions/procedures like:

   ALTER TABLE employees PARALLEL 4
   ALTER Index abs .. PARALLEL 4

☞ QUESTION 79

Invalid object in sys schema

I have the following invalid objects in one of my database's. I tried to recompile them but there is no good results. Do I need to re-run cat patch? If not, how do I make these invalid objects valid?

SYS DBA_LOGSTDBY_LOG VIEW
SYS DBA_LOGSTDBY_PROGRESS VIEW
SYS DBMS_CAPTURE_PROCESS PACKAGE BODY
SYS DBMS_INTERNAL_LOGSTDBY PACKAGE BODY
SYS DBMS_LOGMNR_D PACKAGE BODY
SYS DBMS_LOGMNR_FFVTOLOGMNRT PROCEDURE
SYS DBMS_LOGMNR_OCTOLOGMNRT PROCEDURE
SYS DBMS_LOGMNR_SESSION PACKAGE BODY
SYS DBMS_LOGSTDBY PACKAGE BODY
SYS LOGMNR_DICT_CACHE PACKAGE BODY
SYS LOGMNR_GTLO3 PROCEDURE
SYS LOGMNR_KRVRDA_TEST_APPLY PROCEDURE
SYS LOGMNR_KRVRDLUID3 PROCEDURE
SYS LOGMNR_KRVRDREPDICT3 PROCEDURE

✍ ANSWER

Make sure that all objects being referred by these invalid objects are valid. For example, if a procedure references a column on a table that is no longer available on the table, the procedure will be invalid.

However, since these are SYS objects, and I presume you have not created any tables using the SYS, check your Views.

☞ QUESTION **80**

Getting data in one pass

My inventory table has approximately 30 million records.

These are the columns:

ITEM_NUMBER

INVENTORY_DATE

QTY_AVAILABLE

There is no indexes on this table.

I would like to fetch the following info from this table to a given item number.

```
<OL style="MARGIN-TOP: 0in" type=1>
<LI class=MsoNormal style="MARGIN: 0in 0in 0pt; mso-list:
l0 level1 lfo1; tab-stops: list .5in">Max(QTY_AVAILABLE)
<LI class=MsoNormal style="MARGIN: 0in 0in 0pt; mso-list:
l0 level1 lfo1; tab-stops: list .5in">Min(QTY_AVAILABLE)
<LI class=MsoNormal style="MARGIN: 0in 0in 0pt; mso-list:
l0 level1 lfo1; tab-stops: list .5in">AVG(QTY_AVAILABLE)
<LI class=MsoNormal style="MARGIN: 0in 0in 0pt; mso-
list: l0 level1 lfo1; tab-stops: list .5in">MAX(INVENTORY_
DATE),
<LI class=MsoNormal style="MARGIN: 0in 0in 0pt; mso-list:
l0 level1 lfo1; tab-stops: list .5in">QTY_AVAILABLE when
the INVENTORY_DATE = MAX(INVENTORY_DATE)</OL>
```

I could write two queries, one would fetch the first 4 values,

and the second would fetch the 5th value. However, this
approach would require two full table scans.

What can you suggest for a SQL (or PL/SQL script) that
would select all 5 items within one pass through the data in
the table?

I am using Oracle 9i. Version 9.2.05.0

✍ ANSWER

SQL> CREATE TABLE inventory_table (
  2   item_number   NUMBER
  3 , inventory_date   DATE
  4 , qty_available   NUMBER
  5)
  6 /

Table created.

SQL> INSERT INTO inventory_table
  2 SELECT FLOOR(DBMS_RANDOM.VALUE(1,6))
  3 ,   DBMS_RANDOM.VALUE(1,365)
  4   +
  5   TO_DATE('20031231','YYYYMMDD')
  6 ,   FLOOR(DBMS_RANDOM.VALUE(1,100))
  7 FROM   sys.all_users
  8 WHERE ROWNUM <= 30
  9 /

30 rows created.

SQL> SELECT   invt.item_number
  2 ,   TO_CHAR(invt.inventory_date

```
  3     ,     'fmMM/DD/YYYY HH:fmMI:SS AM') inventory_
dt
  4 ,     invt.qty_available
  5 FROM    inventory_table             invt
  6 ORDER BY invt.item_number
  7 ,       invt.inventory_date
  8 /
```

```
ITEM_NUMBER INVENTORY_DT        QTY_AVAILABLE
----------- -------------------- -----------
          1 3/21/2004 10:10:46 AM        40
          1 5/9/2004 10:19:50 AM         87
          1 6/21/2004 1:06:52 AM         65
          1 8/30/2004 6:10:14 AM         74
          1 12/17/2004 5:18:09 PM        95
          2 4/12/2004 7:11:06 AM         77
          2 7/10/2004 7:07:14 AM         48
          2 8/13/2004 12:44:34 AM        38
          2 11/26/2004 9:41:40 AM        79
          3 2/18/2004 7:50:18 PM         38
          3 8/9/2004 11:46:47 PM         63
          3 10/1/2004 4:58:14 PM         58
          3 10/30/2004 10:45:40 AM       77
          4 1/4/2004 4:19:21 AM          89
          4 1/15/2004 7:19:24 AM         12
          4 2/10/2004 9:29:49 PM         13
          4 5/9/2004 3:55:18 PM          88
          4 5/14/2004 7:51:47 PM         72
          4 5/17/2004 9:44:45 AM         11
          4 5/22/2004 12:05:31 PM        27
          4 8/6/2004 4:52:48 PM          68
          4 10/5/2004 2:10:25 PM          1
          4 11/5/2004 4:17:14 AM         12
          4 11/19/2004 9:29:28 PM        92
          4 12/16/2004 8:29:21 AM        89
```

```
      5 3/18/2004 8:42:33 PM        45
      5 5/12/2004 6:52:46 AM        74
      5 5/30/2004 6:07:00 AM        86
      5 8/10/2004 3:35:24 AM         2
      5 8/16/2004 1:32:11 AM        17
```

30 rows selected.

```
SQL> SELECT   grpd.item_number
  2 ,       grpd.max_qty_avail
  3 ,       grpd.min_qty_avail
  4 ,       grpd.avg_qty_avail
  5 ,         TO_CHAR(TO_DATE(SUBSTR(grpd.max_date_
plus_qty,1,14)
  6            ,      'YYYYMMDDHH24MISS')
  7            ,      'fmMM/DD/YYYY HH:fmMI:SS AM')      max_
inventory_date
  8 ,       TO_NUMBER(SUBSTR(grpd.max_date_plus_qty
  9                  ,    15))              qty_during_max_inv_
date
 10 FROM   (SELECT  invt.item_number
 11      ,      MAX(invt.qty_available)       max_qty_avail
 12      ,      MIN(invt.qty_available)       min_qty_avail
 13      ,      AVG(invt.qty_available)       avg_qty_avail
 14      ,      MAX(TO_CHAR(invt.inventory_date
 15              ,    'YYYYMMDDHH24MISS')
 16           || TO_CHAR(invt.qty_available
 17              ,    'fm000000000'))   max_date_plus_qty
 18      FROM   inventory_table            invt
 19      GROUP BY invt.item_number) grpd
 20 ORDER BY grpd.item_number
 21 /
```

ITEM_NUMBER MAX_QTY_AVAIL MIN_QTY_AVAIL AVG_
QTY_AVAIL MAX_INVENTORY_DATE   QTY_DURING_

MAX_INV_DATE

---------- ----------- ----------- ----------- --------------------- --------------

----

	1	95	40	72.2 12/17/2004 5:18:09 PM
95				
	2	79	38	60.5 11/26/2004 9:41:40 AM
79				
	3	77	38	59 10/30/2004 10:45:40 AM
77				
	4	92	1	47.8333333 12/16/2004 8:29:21
AM		89		
	5	86	2	44.8 8/16/2004 1:32:11 AM
	17			

SQL>

☞ **QUESTION 81**

Replace outer join with union

I need help with replacing an outer join with union, all in a view. How can I replace the following snippet?

```
SELECT *
FROM A_A, B_B
WHERE A_A_DBG = B_B_DBG (+)
AND A_A_AKL = B_B_AKL (+)
AND A_A_KLG = B_B_KLG (+)
AND A_A_BLG = B_B_BLG (+)
```

✐ **ANSWER**

You can try this:

```
CREATE TABLE TB1(A INT,B INT);
CREATE TABLE TB2(A INT,B INT);
SQL817> SELECT * FROM TB1;
A B
--------- ---------
3 3
1 1
2 4
SQL817> SELECT * FROM TB2;
A B
--------- ---------
2 2
4 4
3 3
SQL817> SELECT TB1.A,TB1.B,TO_NUMBER(NULL) A,TO_
```

NUMBER(NULL) B
2 FROM TB1
3 WHERE (A,B) NOT IN (SELECT A,B FROM TB2)
4 UNION ALL
5 SELECT TB1.A,TB1.B,TB2.A,TB2.B
6 FROM TB1,TB2
7 WHERE TB1.A=TB2.A AND TB1.B=TB2.B;
A B A B

--------- --------- --------- ---------

1 1
2 4
3 3 3 3

☞ QUESTION **82**

DML on Global temp table

Does DML's ,on Global Temporary table generate REDO? If
it does, then how do I suppress it?

✐ ANSWER

It does. In 9i, it is supposed to be way less than the regular
table. But it will be generating a enormous amount of redo.
It is a well reported bug (bug# 2874489), and is supposed to
be fixed in 10g.

☞ QUESTION 83

Getting procedure and package names

How can I get the list of procedure names and package name in my database?

✍ ANSWER

SELECT object_name,object_type FROM dba_objects
    WHERE object_type IN ('PROCEDURE','PACKAGE')

☞ QUESTION 84

A long running query in Oracle

How can I find a long running query in Oracle?

✍ ANSWER

You can use something like this:
SELECT *
FROM (SELECT sql_text, elapsed_time AS "Elapsed time (in microseconds)"
FROM sys.v_$sqlarea
ORDER BY elapsed_time DESC)
WHERE rownum < 11
/

☞ QUESTION 85

Execution stats shown on TOAD

When I run up Toad, select tuning, and look up the execution stats for some SQL that was running, there were four values I'm not sure about:

Persistent memory 1424
Sharable memory 13828
Runtime memory 2180
Users opening 0

What do the figures mean? Does 2180 mean milliseconds?

✍ ANSWER

As stated in the Oracle Reference Guide (description of V$SQL):

SHARABLE_MEM = Amount of shared memory used by the child cursor (in bytes).

PERSISTENT_MEM = Fixed amount of memory used for the lifetime of the child cursor (in bytes).

RUNTIME_MEM = Fixed amount of memory required during the execution of the child cursor.

USERS_OPENING = Number of users executing the statement.

☞ QUESTION **86**

Tuning SGA

I installed oracle 8i (1.7) on a windows 2000 advance server. It has a Intel Xeon Processor and 2 GB RAM.

We are running one instance, and the total database size is about 100 GB. We have around 100 active connections.

Now, I want to tune the server parameter, especially SGA.

✎ ANSWER

SGA will be allocated depending upon the behavior of the database.

Based on your table nature, you can split Buffer Cache in:

1. Default buffer cache (as general).
2. Keep buffer pool (for small like master, look up type of tables).
3. Recycle buffer pool (Purging in nature table).

If required, your table space should be designed effectively to restrict fragmentation for purging tables.

☞ **QUESTION 87**

Checking fragmentation

I would like to know the query on how we can find the fragmentation in the table spaces. How can I avoid it, except this query: "alter tablespace tablespace_name coalesce;"?

✍ **ANSWER**

To quick view the TS fragmentation, we can use "DBA_ FREE_SPACE" view.

"alter tablespace coalesce;" is only effective on honey-comb fragmentation. In case of the second one, do the general procedure to import and export.

If your versions support LMT, then use LMT with uniform extent size. It will help to restrict from fragmentation, deletion and rebuild operation.

☞ QUESTION 88

Views or tables

I have a requirement to supply data which requires a large reporting system. Many of the reports take their data from multiple tables with queries that require complex joins and aggregate functions. Also, the volume of data in each table to process is quite large.

All the reports must be accessed using stored procedures from an ASP.Net interface, using ref cursors to pass the report data back.

If creating use views for some of these reports, will it be detrimental to performance? Should I create tables for the final reports that are truncated each time the report has been run?

Is there a better way that I can manage this?

✍ ANSWER

Views can be used to store some complicated queries, but since you use procedures and ref-cursors anyway, that advantage could disappear. It is the data base developer that maintains the query. In general, there is no performance loss in using views.

Filling and especially truncating tables, sounds like a bad idea. If you need to use temporary data, have a look at true temporary tables.

☞ QUESTION **89**

Connecting with oracle database

How can I connect with oracle database?

✎ ANSWER

You can connect with oracle db with "sqlplus" on the server, or on the client under windows "start -> execute -> cmd ->return type : sqlplus login/password@base".

☞ **QUESTION 90**

Sorting results

We have a database that consists of approx 40,000 records. We are supposed to write a search method for it. The searching technique includes finding data on suffixes, prefixes, and in between character combinations. E.g. we have data

fenvia
nerufen
asfenas

Now, if we have to conduct search on keyword 'fen', then it should return all the three records mentioned above in a sequence:

fenvia // like 'fen*'
nerufen // like '*fen'
asfenas // like '*fen*' minus all above records
(to avoid repetition)

How can we speed up our search technique for such bulk with data i.e. 40,000 entries (approx)?

✍ **ANSWER**

Create an oracle text index, (INDEXTYPE IS "ctxsys. context") and select the data using contains in the where clause.

See the Oracle Text Reference Guide for details. .

☞ QUESTION 91

database is full

Can I extend the size of the database when it is full?

✍ ANSWER

You need to add files to the database's table space, or make the existing data files auto extensible.

To add space to a table space:

ALTER TABLESPACE ... ADD DATAFILE ...

To make data files auto extensible:

ALTER DATABASE DATAFILE '...' AUTOEXTEND ON;

BTW: If you don't like commands, you can add space from the Enterprise Manager GUI.

☞ QUESTION 92

Explaining the explain plan

I made an explain plan for this SQL:

 explain plan for SELECT ROUND(AVG(SAMPLE_RESULT.
RESULT),2) avg_result,
AVG(DECODE(SAMPLE.QUALITYSTATUS, 'P', 1,'F', 5))
qltystatus,
TO_CHAR("SAMPLE"."SAMPLEDT",'dd-Mon-yyyy')
sampledt
FROM "SAMPLE","SAMPLE_RESULT","ACTIVITY"
WHERE   "SAMPLE"."SAMPLEID"   =   "SAMPLE_
RESULT"."SAMPLEID"
AND "SAMPLE_RESULT"."TESTINSTANCE" = fn_max_
instance (sample.sampleid, sample_result.testid, sample_
result.propertyid)
AND   "SAMPLE"."ACTIVITYID"   =
"ACTIVITY"."ACTIVITYID"
AND ACTIVITY.LOCATIONID = 'S5003C'
AND SAMPLE.EVENTID <> 'AD-HOC'
AND "SAMPLE"."SAMPLESTATUS" = 'L'
AND   TO_DATE(TO_CHAR(SAMPLE.SAMPLEDT,'dd-mon-
yyyy')) BETWEEN '01-Jan-2003' AND '07-Jan-2003'
AND SAMPLE_RESULT.PROPERTYID = 'GCV'
GROUP BY TO_CHAR("SAMPLE"."SAMPLEDT",'dd-Mon-
yyyy')

and I got this result:

PLAN_TABLE_OUTPUT

```
-------------------------------------------------------
| Id | Operation | Name | Rows | Bytes | Cost |
-------------------------------------------------------
| 0 | SELECT STATEMENT | | 1 | 78 | 11 |
| 1 | SORT GROUP BY | | 1 | 78 | 11 |
|* 2 | FILTER | | | | |
|* 3 | TABLE ACCESS BY INDEX ROWID | SAMPLE_RESULT
| 20469 | 619K| 2 |
| 4 | NESTED LOOPS | | 1 | 78 | 9 |
| 5 | NESTED LOOPS | | 2 | 94 | 5 |
| 6 | TABLE ACCESS BY INDEX ROWID| ACTIVITY | 1 | 15 |
3 |
|* 7 | INDEX RANGE SCAN | IDX_ACTIVITY_LOCATION | 1
| | 1 |
|* 8 | TABLE ACCESS BY INDEX ROWID| SAMPLE | 2 | 64 |
2 |
|* 9 | INDEX RANGE SCAN | KSAMPLE_ACTIVITYID | 366 |
| 1 |
|* 10 | INDEX RANGE SCAN | SAMPLE_RESULT_IDX_003 |
1 | | 1 |
-------------------------------------------------------
```

Predicate Information (identified by operation id):
```
---------------------------------------------
```

2   -   filter(TO_DATE('01-Jan-2003')<=TO_DATE('07-Jan-2003'))
3   -   filter("SAMPLE_RESULT"."TESTINSTANCE"="LVL_
GPP"."FN_MAX_INSTANCE"("SAMPLE"."SAMPL
EID","SAMPLE_RESULT"."TESTID","SAMPLE_
RESULT"."PROPERTYID"))
7 - access("ACTIVITY"."LOCATIONID"='S5003C')
8   -   filter("SAMPLE"."EVENTID"<>'AD-HOC' AND TO_
DATE(TO_CHAR("SAMPLE"."SAMPLEDT",'dd-m
on-yyyy'))>='01-Jan-2003' AND TO_DATE(TO_CHAR("SAM

PLE"."SAMPLEDT",'dd-mon-
yyyy'))<='07-Jan-2003')
9 - access ("SAMPLE"."ACTIVITYID"="ACTIVITY"."ACTIVIT
YID" AND "SAMPLE"."SAMPLESTATUS"=
'L')
10 - access ("SAMPLE"."SAMPLEID"="SAMPLE_
RESULT"."SAMPLEID" AND "SAMPLE_RESULT"."PROPER
TYID"='GCV')
filter("SAMPLE_RESULT"."PROPERTYID"='GCV')

Note: cpu costing is off

34 rows selected.

****

What should I do to shorten the time since the query takes
more than half an hour to complete?

✍ ANSWER

First of all, if possible take the logic from your "fn_max_
instance" function and embed it within your SQL statement.
Context switching between PL/SQL and SQL can be costly.

Second, it looks like your "sample.sampledt" column has a
data type of date. Then, this predicate:

AND TO_DATE(TO_CHAR(SAMPLE.SAMPLEDT,'dd-mon-
yyyy')) BETWEEN '01-Jan-2003' AND '07-Jan-2003'

Should instead read:

AND sample.sampledt BETWEEN TO_DATE('01-Jan-2003','DD-Mon-YYYY') AND TO_DATE('07-Jan-2003','DD-Mon-YYYY')

You should only compare date to dates, number to numbers, and strings to strings.

☞ QUESTION 93

Session related queries

Can you tell me how to find SQL statements by specific session, using session id and not by using "parsing_user_id"?

✍ ANSWER

Oracle associates sessions with statements for open cursors (V$OPEN_CURSOR), but also keeps track of the last and current SQL statement for each session (V$SESSION.SQL_ID and PREV_SQL_ID).

Here are a couple of queries you can try:

Session 1:
SQL> SELECT USERENV('SESSIONID') FROM dual;
USERENV('SESSIONID')

97
 Session 2:
SQL> SELECT sql_text AS "OPEN CURSORS"
2 FROM v_$open_cursor o, v_$session s
3 WHERE o.saddr = s.saddr
4 AND s.audsid = 97
5 /

OPEN CURSORS

SELECT USERENV('SESSIONID') FROM dual

SQL> SELECT sql_text AS "LAST SQL EXECUTED"

2 FROM v$sqltext t, v$session s

2 WHERE s.audsid = 97

3 AND s.sql_id = t.sql_id

4 /

LAST SQL EXECUTED

SELECT USERENV('SESSIONID') FROM dual

☞ QUESTION 94

Oracle 8/9/10 performance problem

I have a problem on trying to test a piece of software that heavily relies on an Oracle Database. The last version of the software was working fine, but now it is very slow, and sometimes completely unresponsive. It seems that the database is taking a very long time replying to adds/deletes/query's.

Is there any way I can somehow put the database into 'debug' mode where it will create a log file of what it is doing?

We have Oracle 8i, 9i and 10g.

✑ ANSWER

You should take a look at the documentation.

Here are a couple of things that you can do:

First, enable session tracing. Start a session in your application. Find out the Sid and serial for your session and use "dbms_system.set_sql_trace_in_session" for that session to true. Now all statements executed from this session are written to a trace-file, along with the time needed to parse, execute and fetch. Also, the needed logical and physical I/O are stored. You can find this file in the user-dump directory. To find out where that is, give the following command in sqlplus: "show parameter user_dump_dest". Close your session. Go to the directory (on the db-server) indicated by the "user_dump_dest" and look for your trace file. This trace file can be formatted using 'tkprof'. This is a standard Oracle tool:

"tkprof   <<z>tracefile>   <<z>outputfile>   sys=no sort=prsela,fchela exeela"

This will sort the file and put the statements that took the longest time on top.

Secondly, you can use Statspack. This will monitor your entire database instead of just 1 session, more info will be stored than by tracing.

☞ **QUESTION 95**

10g Advisor

I am trying to generate recommendations for indexes using Oracle's 10g advisors. However, I don't have access to the Enterprise Manager. I am doing it by using the "DBMS_ Advisor" package and "SQL*Plus(Pl/Sql)". I am getting recommendations, but only for materialized views. I am trying to get the advisor to recommend indexes.

The default is that it will recommend both. However, I am wondering if there is a setting or parameter that I can change to force it to recommend indexes?

Below is a sample of the code that is only generating materialized views. I have four tables, 2 with 100,000 rows and 2 with 50,000 rows, all with primary keys and foreign keys.

```
DECLARE

task_desc VARCHAR2(100);
task_id NUMBER;
task_name VARCHAR2(30);
workload_name VARCHAR2(30);

BEGIN

task_name := 'Task_mag';

dbms_advisor.create_task (DBMS_ADVISOR.SQLACCESS_
ADVISOR,
task_id, task_name, 'My Advisor Task', DBMS_ADVISOR.
```

SQLACCESS_WAREHOUSE);

dbms_advisor.set_task_parameter   ('Task_mag',
'EVALUATION_ONLY', 'FALSE');
DBMS_OUTPUT.PUT_LINE('test3');

dbms_advisor.set_task_parameter   ('Task_mag',
'EXECUTION_TYPE', 'FULL');
DBMS_OUTPUT.PUT_LINE('test4');

-- create the workload
workload_name :='Workload_mv';

dbms_advisor.create_sqlwkld(workload_name,   'MV
workload' , NULL);

-- now link the two together

dbms_advisor.add_sqlwkld_ref(task_name,   workload_
name) ;

-- add a SQL statement

dbms_advisor.add_sqlwkld_statement   (workload_
name,'App','action', NULL,15,3000,423,507,60,704, 3,'16-FEB-
2002',80, 'test','SELECT test.t2.fname2 as T2fname, test.
t2.lname2 as T2LastN, test.t3.fname3 as T3FirstN from test.
t2, test.t3 where (test.t2.primk = 84756) and (test.t3.primk =
222)');

DBMS_ADVISOR.EXECUTE_TASK(task_name);

DBMS_ADVISOR.CREATE_FILE(DBMS_ADVISOR.GET_

TASK_SCRIPT(task_name),
'MY_DIR','script66.sql');

END;
/

✍ ANSWER

Try to use "DBMS_ADVISOR.SQLACCESS_OLTP" instead of
"DBMS_ADVISOR.SQLACCESS_WAREHOUSE".

☞ QUESTION 96

Main use of Pmon

What is the main use of Pmon?

✍ ANSWER

The process monitor performs process recovery when a user
process fails. PMON is responsible for cleaning up the cache
and freeing resources that the process was using. PMON also
checks on the dispatcher processes and server processes,
and restarts them if they failed.

☞ QUESTION 97

Analyzing SQL query

When a SQL is given, how can I analyze it?

✍ ANSWER

Identify the writing of SQL. A bad written SQL will never give you a good result. If you feel that some changes are required, do them.

After that, identify the execution plan of the query for index usage and full table scan etc. My statement for index usage doesn't mean that index scan is better than full table scan.

You identify the Cost, Card, and Bytes fetched by the query, and proceed further for tuning them.

☞ QUESTION 98

Recovery in occurrence of crash instance

Is recovery possible when instance crash occurs?

✍ ANSWER

Oracle will do instance recovery when you restart the instance after failure. If you use RAC, the surviving instances will do the instance recovery when the failure is detected. So, either way, Oracle should do it automatically. If it cannot, a DBA will have to intervene.

☞ QUESTION 99

Does remote table use remote indexes?

I'm tuning a SQL query like this:

Select (...) FROM owner.table1@remotebase TAB1

and I want to HINT with "index_combine",

Select /*+ index_combine (tab1) (...) FROM owner.
table1@remotebase TAB1

My question is, would it use remote indexes?

Or should I place something like this?

Select /*+ index(tab1 Owner.tab1_index01@remotebase
Owner.tab1_index02@remotebase   Owner.
tab1_index03@remotebase)   (...)/*   FROM   owner.
table1@remotebase TAB1

✍ ANSWER

You can try this:

Select /*+ index_combine (tab1) (...) FROM owner.
table1@remotebase TAB1

You can also try "*+DRVING_SITE( )*" hint on the remote
table in the query.

☞ QUESTION 100

Analyze table frequently

Is there any harm analyzing a table more than once a day?

I have four tables of about 3 Million records which are queried heavily. There are some inserts into these tables every now and then.

I usually do analyze after every DML. Each DML affects about 15000 records at a time. It takes about 6 minutes at the most and 45 seconds at the least to analyze.

Is there a problem if I analyze frequently?

I have an IOT with zero records. Why does it take a long time to analyze that?

✍ ANSWER

After analyze, it is expected that all queries in the shared pool that touched the analyzed table are invalidated. This would mean that Oracle has to parse them again to recalculate the execution plan. This would cause a decrease in performance. If the distribution of your data does not radically change, there would be no need to analyze after each DML operation.

INDEX

'cpu_time'...149

'pctfree' 78

'pstart'...145

'pstop' 145

'TK*Prof' 61

'tkprof'...140

"*+DRVING_SITE( )*" hint..207

"ALTER TABLE" command 1

"arrival_groups_id"..57

"Backup/OS limit/oracle" configurations...........................49

"ctxsys.context"..192

"DBMS_Advisor" package 202

"EXCHANGE PARTITION" 1

"fn_max_instance" function...196

"no_invalidations" parameter 71

"parsing_user_id"..198

"PGA RAM / TEMP" space..66

"PX server shutdown"...90

"RMA_LINES_EXT" table..170

"SHRINK" clause..1

"slave shutdown wait"...90

"SQL*Scratchpad" tool...16

"SQL*Trace" 1

"TK*Prof" 1

10g Advisor...202

10gR1..115

10gR1 docs...90

146GB SCSI disks 141

3rd party application 81

5th value...180

9iR2...115

ACL table 112

ACL table index 114

active connections..188

actual data distribution...52

actual key value 91

Aggregate function 21, 190

aggregate max 21

AIX..128

alert log 99

Alphanumeric data type..3

ALTER SESSION..100

Analytic function 21

analytic query..21

analyzed table 142

ANSI JOINS 39

application connectivity 128

application tuning...78

application's nature 81

archive files disk 128
Archive log 128
ASM 77
ASP.Net interface 190
ASSM 42
AUM 76
auto extensible 193
auto trace 121
auto update stats options 37
AWR 62
bad set up 33
Bad view 33
Batch loading 126
Batch tuning 126
behavior of the database 188
bind values 24
bind variable 45
bind variable problem 23
bit flag PUBLIC/PRIVATE 112
BIT map indexes 47
bitmap index 117
blocks in consistent mode 13
blocks in current mode 13
bounce the DB 147
buffer Hit ratio 6
buffer pool 188
bug 137
bug# 2874489 185
bulk collect feature 80

cache database 110

Card 205

cardinality 57

cat patch 178

CBO 18, 24, 41, 75

character combinations 192

Checkpoint 99

cloning 105

coalesce 189

Commit Time 22

Commit time format 22

compared schema 69

comparison operation 3

complex joins 190

complicated queries 190

composite bitmap 119

Composite bitmap indexes 117

Composite Index 4, 25, 41

compute statistics 140

concurrent sessions 147

connectivity 128

consistent get mechanism 175

Consistent gets 13

consistent mode 175

constant predicates 46

contained indexed columns 51

Context switching 80, 196

continuous ping 128

cost-based optimizer 12

cpu costing 196

crash instance 206

create functional index 23

current environment 6

Cursor performance issue 129

Custom Scripts 106

custom solution 20

data base developer 190

Data warehouse type environment 17

database TEST 67

database vendor 106

db block gets 13

DB cache 45

DB server 128

Db2 approach 37

DB2 Databases 16

DBlink 67

dbms_stats 17, 132

dBWR 99

ddl 140

'debug' mode 200

default optimizer_mode 100

default snapshot interval 62

degree of parallelism 176

dictionary tables 176

dirty buffers 99

Disk partition strategy 141

disk space 111

DML 14

DML operation 208
DMT...50, 63
document ID..112
Document security model 112
driving table...12
duplicate values 19
dynamic sampling...110
dynamic SQL 24
Enterprise Manager..202
Enterprise Manager GUI..193
ErWin..69
etalon..69
EXECUTE IMMEDIATE 24
execution method...58
execution plan..170
execution statistics..13
Execution stats 187
existing structures...147
Explain Plan 16, 51, 75, 83, 140
extremely high transaction system 176
filter conditions...12
Forced view..115
Foreign key..106
Foreign Keys 54
foreign-key in application..106
fragmentation...105, 188, 189
free size 42
frequency 99
FTS 34

FULL hint...64
Full table scan..................................36, 57, 107, 173
function base index...91
Functional index...23
function-based index...19
functions...166
gather stats time..17
Getting procedure..186
Global temp table..185
GMT...22
hash join..64
hash outer join...64
hash partitioned table...145
hash partitioning...145
high I/O..77
high I/O activity...81
high watermark..136
hints...47
honey-comb fragmentation...189
HP UNIX...128
HWM..50
HWM problem..1
id column...12
implicit cursor..130
index..4
index access..82
index access costs...66
index block...82
Index partition..124

Index scans...3, 205

indexed columns..51

Indexes Difference 67

Initran...77

inline view 21, 166

inner join query with partitioning...39

inner query..166

insert intensive..19

inserts..208

instance recovery 206

instance tuning..78

internal algorithm 146

Invalid object...178

inventory table 179

IOT..208

Join Order...41

Julian time 22

latch/enqueue level..82

Library cache latch...8

list partitioning..145

listener 127

LMT..50, 63

load tests..105

lock_sga parameter 138

logging...43

logical i/o's...13

long running query...186

loopholes 147

looping constructs..80

lower I/O 81

manual segment space management......................78

materialized view optimizer..................................31

Materialized views......................................31, 33

MAX(ID)...20

maximum size of SGA..131

Maxtran...77

mdac..127

measures of performance....................................131

modification processes..82

Mount Point Structure of Filesystem...............125

multi-part keys...1

multiple processors..176

multi-restrictio..41

navigation PREV/NEXT Page.............................112

nested loops 66

new dump 147

no_index optimizer hint....................................143

None force 115

NT server 6

Numeric 3

nvl..166

object statistics...37

odbc...127

OLTP environment 17

open cursors...198

Operating System Redhat Linux 2.4.9...............49

optimal 99, 136

optimal execution plan 75

optimal plans 46
optimal SQL 46
'optimized' query 75
optimized SQL 75
optimizer 170
optimizer goal default 123
optimizer parameters 66
optimizer_mode 100
optimizing/tuning RDBMS 16
OR operations 113
ORA-01594 135
ORA-01595 135
ora-02287 sequence 149
ORA-024012 7
Oracle BUG 642267 138
oracle dictionary table 124
Oracle Enterprise Manager 16
oracle mount point 49
Oracle Reference Guide 187
Oracle server information 125
oracle text index 192
Oracle: 8 137
Original Rows 17
outer join 20, 184
outer query 166
package name 186
parallel capability 176
parallel execution slaves 90
Parallel hint 176

parallel servers..176
PARSE..24
parsed query plans..71
partition 1, 145
PCTfree..77
performance degradation 120
performance investigation..113
performance problem 200
Performance tuning..151
Persistent memory 1424..187
physical model 69
physical query syntax..75
PK constraint..19
plan invalidations 71
plan table 56
Pmon..204
Predicate Information..195
Primary Key..54, 108
procedure names 186
Procedure tuning..80
process monitor..204
process recovery..204
Production database 8, 105
Proper index..54
Purging..188
QA..67
query performance 31
Query tuning with NVL 96
RAC 206

RAID controller...141

RAM...131

rank() over...21

rdbms/admin 7

Recovery..206

recursive transaction 135

REDO 185

ref-cursors 190

regular index 91

Relational databases 106

remote indexes 207

remote table 207

reporting system 190

retention table..22

role...100

Rollback segment error 135

rollback space 78

rollbacks the transaction, undo segment 76

Runtime memory 2180 187

S.A.M.E. Stripe and Mirror Everything 141

s_con 34

SAP R/3 4.7 Enterprise edition..49

scheduled online rebuild 50

SCN (System Change Number)..175

SCOTT..68

search method..192

search technique..192

security model pattern..113

Select doubt..12

select statement..19, 58
selection statement 39
server parameter..188
Session related queries 198
session tracing 200
session wise...148
SGA..77, 131, 188
Sharable memory 13828....................................187
shared pool..208
Shrinking index table space 42
Sid and serial..200
Single column indexes 5
slow reports..33
slow response 47
snapshot timing..44
Solaris: 2.8 137
Spot Light on Oracle...16
SQL Navigator 16
SQL query 4, 205
SQL Reference Guide...75
SQL trace dump 140
SQL*Loader 19
sqlplus 191
StatPack...77
Statspack reports..8, 44, 109
statspack snapshots 148
statspack.snap..44
summation...39
SYS objects 178

sys schema...178

Table scan...1, 51

table stats...132

tablespace PSAPPML...49

target host...127

temporary tablespace...63

TEST...68

test environment..37

timed tests 103

time-sensitive histograms..38

TOAD..16, 187

trace analysis...109

transactional index..82

truncating tables 190

TS fragmentation 189

tune...48

Tuning 39, 54

Tuning buffer hit ratio 6

Tuning SGA...188

Tuning SQL...83

tuning techniques 136

Twisted Nail...128

type of index...139

unanalyzed tables 123

undo segment header block 22

uniform extent size..189

union 184

UNION ALL...34

Unique constraint 19

unique index...19

user-accessible front-end...46

USERDATA parallel...43

utlxplan.sql 7

VB application..127

Visual Explain 16

VPD..113

Windows XP 10gR1...138

wrapper procedure...58

Attention SAP Experts

Have you ever considered writing a book in your area of SAP? Equity Press is the leading provider of knowledge products in SAP applications consulting, development, and support. If you have a manuscript or an idea of a manuscript, we'd love to help you get it published!

Please send your manuscript or manuscript ideas to jim@sapcookbook.com – we'll help you turn your dream into a reality.

Or mail your inquiries to:

Equity Press Manuscripts
BOX 706
Riverside, California
92502

Tel (951)788-0810
Fax (951)788-0812

50% Off your next
SAPCOOKBOOK order

If you plan of placing an order for 10 or more books from www.sapcookbook.com you qualify for volume discounts. Please send an email to books@sapcookbook.com or phone 951-788-0810 to place your order.

You can also fax your orders to 951-788-0812 .

Interview books are great for cross-training

In the new global economy, the more you know the better. The sharpest consultants are doing everything they can to pick up more than one functional area of SAP. Each of the following Certification Review / Interview Question books provides an excellent starting point for your module learning and investigation. These books get you started like no other book can – by providing you the information that you really need to know, and fast.

SAPCOOKBOOK Interview Questions, Answers, and Explanations

ABAP	-	SAP ABAP Certification Review: SAP ABAP Interview Questions, Answers, and Explanations
SD	-	SAP SD Interview Questions, Answers, and Explanations
Security	-	SAP Security: SAP Security Essentials
HR	-	mySAP HR Interview Questions, Answers, and Explanations: SAP HR Certification Review
BW	-	SAP BW Ultimate Interview Questions, Answers, and Explanations: SAW BW Certification Review
	-	SAP SRM Interview Questions Answers and Explanations
Basis	-	SAP Basis Certification Questions: Basis Interview Questions, Answers, and Explanations
MM	-	SAP MM Certification and Interview Questions: SAP MM Interview Questions, Answers, and Explanations

SAP BW Ultimate Interview Questions, Answers, and Explanations

Key Topics Include:

- The most important BW settings to know
- BW tables and transaction code quick references
- Certification Examination Questions
- Extraction, Modeling and Configuration
- Transformations and Administration
- Performance Tuning, Tips & Tricks, and FAQ
- Everything a BW resource needs to know before an interview

mySAP HR Interview Questions, Answers, and Explanations

Key topics include:

- The most important HR settings to know
- mySAP HR Administration tables and transaction code quick references
- SAP HR Certification Examination Questions
- Org plan, Compensation, Year End, Wages, and Taxes
- User Management, Transport System, Patches, and Upgrades
- Benefits, Holidays, Payroll, and Infotypes
- Everything an HR resource needs to know before an interview

SAP SRM Interview Questions, Answers, and Explanations

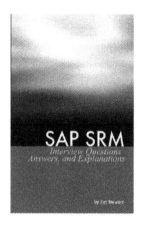

Key Topics Include:

- The most important SRM Configuration to know
- Common EBP Implementation Scenarios
- Purchasing Document Approval Processes
- Supplier Self Registration and Self Service (SUS)
- Live Auctions and Bidding Engine, RFX Processes (LAC)
- Details for Business Intelligence and Spend Analysis
- EBP Technical and Troubleshooting Information

SAP MM Interview Questions, Answers, and Explanations

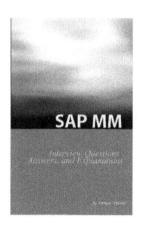

- The most important MM Configuration to know
- Common MM Implementation Scenarios
- MM Certification Exam Questions
- Consumption Based Planning
- Warehouse Management
- Material Master Creation and Planning
- Purchasing Document Inforecords

SAP SD Interview Questions, Answers, and Explanations

- The most important SD settings to know
- SAP SD administration tables and transaction code quick references
- SAP SD Certification Examination Questions
- Sales Organization and Document Flow Introduction
- Partner Procedures, Backorder Processing, Sales BOM
- Backorder Processing, Third Party Ordering, Rebates and Refunds
- Everything an SD resource needs to know before an interview

SAP Basis Interview Questions, Answers, and Explanations

- The most important Basis settings to know
- Basis Administration tables and transaction code quick references
- Certification Examination Questions
- Oracle database, UNIX, and MS Windows Technical Information
- User Management, Transport System, Patches, and Upgrades
- Backup and Restore, Archiving, Disaster Recover, and Security
- Everything a Basis resource needs to know before an interview

SAP Security Essentials

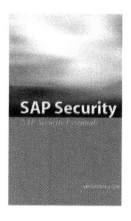

- Finding Audit Critical Combinations
- Authentication, Transaction Logging, and Passwords
- Roles, Profiles, and User Management
- ITAR, DCAA, DCMA, and Audit Requirements
- The most important security settings to know
- Security Tuning, Tips & Tricks, and FAQ
- Transaction code list and table name references

SAP Workflow Interview Questions, Answers, and Explanations

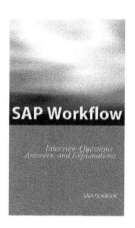

- Database Updates and Changing the Standard
- List Processing, Internal Tables, and ALV Grid Control
- Dialog Programming, ABAP Objects
- Data Transfer, Basis Administration
- ABAP Development reference updated for 2006!
- Everything an ABAP resource needs to know before an interview